DEMYSTIFYING
THE LAW

AN INTRODUCTION FOR
PROFESSIONALS

DANIEL A. BRONSTEIN

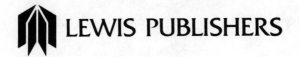 LEWIS PUBLISHERS

Library of Congress Cataloging-in-Publication Data

Bronstein, Daniel A.
    Demystifying the law: an introduction for professionals /
    Daniel A. Bronstein.
        p.   cm.
    Includes bibliographical references and index.
    ISBN 0-87371-324-9
    1. Law—United States.   I. Title.
KF385.B76   1990
349.73—dc20   90-39770
[347.3]   CIP

LEWIS PUBLISHERS, INC.
121 South Main Street, P.O. Drawer 519, Chelsea, Michigan 48118

PRINTED IN THE UNITED STATES OF AMERICA

Dedication

To my wife
Leona Bartel Bronstein
and
In memory of
My grandfather, Arthur C. Mandel, Esq. (1880—1958), of the New
York Bar, who introduced me to the joys and sorrows of logical
argumentation at a very early age
and
My father, Lewis H. Bronstein, M.D., F.A.C.P. (1909—1970), who
transmitted to me his own interest in the problem of the complicated
interactions of law and science.

Introduction

This book is designed to provide the nonlawyer professional with an introduction to the general legal system of the United States. It was originally intended to be part of the publisher's Environmental Law series, but is now aimed for a broader audience. The book is not intended to serve as a legal dictionary; there are many of these already available. It is intended to present some very important legal concepts in their proper context, not as abstract definitions. Readers will not "become lawyers" but will, hopefully, acquire the background necessary to understand and carry on intelligent conversations with lawyers when the need arises.

Part I briefly reviews the basics of the U.S. legal system and gives additional information about it. Some readers may remember some of this material from secondary school or college classes, but it is the author's belief, based on 18 years of university teaching of professional and graduate students, that this brief review will be helpful to all.

Part II discusses some problems that are fundamental, but not unique, to some of the general issues that professionals get involved with. Many of these fall into the general branch of law known as administrative law. This part discusses the general principles of administrative law such as the functions of the *Federal Register*, the Code of Federal Regulations, administrative law judges, etc. It also provides a brief introduction to several very technical issues involving when courts will hear cases.

Part III discusses other legal concepts that can arise in nonadministrative legal cases. These are generally cases between private parties or between the government as an enforcing entity and a private party. The intent, again, is to provide background to the legal setting, not to discuss specific statutes which, in that the case of environmental issues, are or will be covered by other titles in this series and, for other types of issues, are detailed in many other sources.

Throughout the book the references to legal material are given in standard legal citation form. This is done so that the reader can gain some familiarity with the appearance of such citations. An introduction to this citation format is presented in Appendix A under "How to Find It — The Basics of Legal Citation."

I wish to acknowledge the help of the generation of students who have listened to me lecture about these subjects; my colleagues in the Department of Resource Development at Michigan State University, particularly Drs. Frank A. Fear and Milton H. Steinmueller, who looked at parts of this manuscript and made suggestions (some of which I have actually adopted); and my secretary, Ms. Nora Harrison, who has suffered through my sometimes trivial revisions, not to mention having to decipher my chicken scratchings.

Daniel A. Bronstein, S.J.D., is a professor at Michigan State University, East Lansing, Michigan, where he teaches environmental law in the College of Agriculture and Natural Resources, and law, medicine, and public health in the College of Human Medicine. He received his Bachelor of Arts in biophysics from the Johns Hopkins University, Baltimore, Maryland, and his Bachelor of Law from the University of Maryland, College Park, Maryland. After practicing trial law in his native Baltimore for 5 years, he decided to go into teaching and received His Master of Laws and Doctor of Jurisprudential Science degrees from the University of Michigan. He has been at Michigan State University since 1972.

Professor Bronstein is admitted to practice in both Maryland and Michigan. He has served as Chair of Committee on Environmental Law of the American Bar Association, is currently a Vice-Chair of the Committee on Toxic and Hazardous Torts, and has held numerous other committee appointments. He is a member of the Board of Directors of the International Society for Risk Analysis to the American Bar Association, and is also a member of the AAAS, the New York Academy of Sciences, and the Society for the History of Technology.

Contents

PART I
The American Legal System
The Role of Law in Society

PART II
Administrative Law and Judicial Review

PART I

The American Legal System

THE ROLE OF LAW IN SOCIETY

All societies and cultures that anthropologists have studied have laws. Obviously, then, laws do not have to be written; they can be merely understood and passed down from generation to generation as "tradition." The classic example of this in our culture, of course, is the Ten Commandments.

Law, then, is nothing more than the system that is used for regulating the relationships between individuals or groups of individuals in a given culture. There is nothing in the term that implies that the rules that are used will be "fair," "just," or "equitable." This concept can be illuminated by the analogy, "law is to justice as medicine is to health." This means that if all people were healthy there would be no need for the profession of medicine, for doctors, or for anything to aid the sick, because there would be no sick people. Similarly, if we lived in an entirely just society, there would be no reason to have laws or lawyers. However, we do not live in a just society, any more than we are all healthy. Therefore there is a very major need for law and lawyers to organize the affairs of society so that we do not go out and kill one another randomly.

This is not to say, of course, that one cannot hope that, as time goes on, the laws in our society will not become more "just" or "equitable"; certainly we all hope that. Nevertheless, achieving justice or equity is not the aim or role of law. The aim and role of law is to regulate and order the relationships among people and organizations.

1

Sources of American Law

There are four major sources of U.S. law. These are the Constitution of the United States and, of course, of the individual states; treaties made by the U.S. government with foreign countries; statutes passed by Congress or the state legislatures; and court decisions.

1.1 THE CONSTITUTION

The Constitution of the United States is "the supreme law of the land." It is on this basis that statutes, both federal and state, can be declared "unconstitutional" by the courts. If they contradict the Constitution and the Constitution is the "supreme law of the land," then, obviously, the statutes are invalid because they are in violation of the supreme law. The Constitution, of course, like treaties and statutes, is nothing but a set of words on paper; the words have no intrinsic meaning, and we only learn how these words shall be interpreted when we look at court decisions, which tell us what the Constitution means in individual cases.

1.2 TREATIES

Treaties made between the United States and other countries are, according to the Constitution, also part of the law of the land. Treaties are negotiated between the executive branch (the President, Secretary of State, etc.) and foreign governments, and then ratified by the U.S. Senate.

Under the treaty power of the Constitution, the federal government can do things that it cannot do under other powers of the Constitution. For example, duck (and other migratory bird) hunting is regulated by the federal government pursuant to the treaty of 1916 between the United States and Great Britain (on behalf of Canada) called the Migratory Bird Treaty. This treaty was especially negotiated by the government in order to evade a ruling handed down several years earlier, which held that the federal government did not have the authority to control the hunting of migratory birds and that this was an exclusive power of the states.[1] By negotiating a treaty regarding migratory birds, Congress managed to acquire the power to regulate their hunting or, at least, so said the Supreme Court when it decided the issue.[2] In this way, the treaty power is, to some extent, superior to the normal legislative powers of the Congress.

1.3 STATUTES

Federal statutes, of course, are bills enacted by the House of Representatives and the Senate, and then signed by the President. State statutes work the same way, i.e., they are passed by the legislature of a state and signed by the governor thereof.

Under the Constitution the federal government has only "limited" statutory power. *Limited* in the last sentence was put in quotes because, although this is the theoretical statement, in practice the federal government's power to pass statutes appears virtually unlimited. The broadest of the powers of the federal government is to "regulate commerce with foreign Nations and among the several States," the so-called commerce clause. Under this clause the powers of the federal government are extremely broad; it is pursuant to these powers, for example, that the Clean Air Act; the Water Pollution Act; the Food, Drug and Cosmetic Act; the pesticide laws; and all other environmental statutes were passed.

The full extent of the commerce clause today has never been delineated. The most expansive reading to date is in the Supreme Court's decision upholding the equal accommodations section of the Civil Rights Act of 1964. In order to give this act the broadest possible reach, Congress passed it pursuant to the commerce clause, not pursuant to some other section, as one might expect. The case upholding this statute was *Katzenbach v. McClung*, which held that the United States could bring action against "Big Ollie" McClung's Barbecue in Birmingham, Alabama, a very small business that had a minimal number of employees and, in fact, did not even buy its meat or vegetables in interstate commerce. The Supreme Court upheld the regulation of "Big Ollie's" Barbecue on the grounds that (1) although Big Ollie had not bought the food in interstate commerce, his supplier had, and (2) the business was located 11 blocks off of a U.S. highway and therefore travelers who were in interstate travel might end up at "Big Ollie's" seeking food. On this basis, the Supreme Court held that Big Ollie could not refuse to serve blacks.[3]

1.4 COURT DECISIONS

The Constitution, treaties, and statutes are all, as mentioned above, simply words on paper. The interpretation of these words in "real world" situations is the role of courts. One of the great *non sequiturs* of recent political discourse was a statement allegedly made by Barry Goldwater when he was running for President in 1964: "I do not want a Supreme Court which interprets the Constitution, I want a Supreme Court that simply reads what is there."[4] This is a meaningless statement. If you look in the dictionary you will find that *read* and *interpret* are synonymous; it is impossible to do one without doing the other. What Goldwater meant, of course, was something along the lines of "I want a Supreme Court that interprets the Constitution in the same way that I interpret the Constitution," a perfectly valid and rational statement.

Another classic example of the need to consult court decisions in order to understand what words mean is presented by the First Amendment to the U.S. Constitution, which says, in part, "Congress shall make no law restricting ... freedom of speech or of the press." Notice that this says nothing about "except in cases of obscenity," "except in cases of pornography," "except in cases of national security," or "except in cases of sedition"; it says "Congress shall make no law." In fact, if one goes back and looks at Jefferson's and Madison's papers, letters, and diaries it becomes obvious that when they wrote "Congress shall make no law" they meant exactly that — **Congress shall make no law**. However, it has never been interpreted that way. As early as 1798, the courts upheld the Alien and Sedition Acts, which clearly, by any rational reading, put some limitations on freedom of speech and the press.[5]

Thus, in order to really understand what a statute, treaty, or the Constitution means, it is necessary to examine the court decisions that have interpreted that writing.

REFERENCES

1. *U.S. v. McCullagh*, 221 Fed. Rep. 288 (1912).
2. *Missouri v. Holland*, 252 U.S. 416 (1920).
3. 379 U.S. 294 (1964).
4. Allegedly, because Rovere, *The Goldwater Caper*, p. 50 (1965) is the closest to it I have ever found.
5. See Gobel, *History of the Supreme Court of the U.S.: Antecedents and Beginnings to 1801*, pp. 633—654 (1971).

2

The Structure of the Court System

Courts, as we discussed above, are very important, as they tell us what the words in the statute, treaty, or Constitution mean. Therefore, we shall now take a look at the basic outline of a court system.

Looking at Figures 2.1 and 2.2, one can see that the general outlines of the federal and state systems are very similar. Both, typically, have the four-tiered structure indicated. The federal system changed to the current form of this structure in 1924, and the states have, by now, almost all copied it.

2.1 COURTS OF LIMITED JURISDICTION

At the bottom of the ladder are the courts of limited jurisdiction. They are so called because they can only hear those cases that the legislature has given them power to hear. As they are at the bottom of the court structure, appeals are taken from them to the next level.

A bottom court in the federal system (Figure 2.1) is listed as the Federal Magistrate. Federal Magistrates can hear minor federal criminal cases, probable cause hearings in major federal criminal cases, and can sit in for federal district judges if the parties agree to the substitution. The Federal Magistrates are not the only limited-jurisdiction federal court; the best known limited-jurisdiction federal court is Bankruptcy Court, which, as the name implies, has power to hear only bankruptcy cases.

At the bottom of the state system, and here we are using Michigan as a typical system, is the District Court. District Court hears minor criminal cases and also has small claims jurisdiction in civil cases. It is not the only limited-jurisdiction state court; in the Michigan system, as in most states, there is also a court that has power only over estates and

7

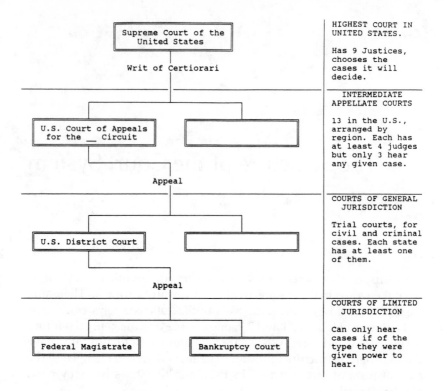

Figure 2.1 Federal courts.

trusts, probate of wills, juvenile criminal cases, and the fate of people who are alleged to be mentally incompetent (Probate Court). Other states recognize their courts of limited jurisdiction by other titles.

2.2 COURTS OF GENERAL JURISDICTION

This is the next level of court above courts of limited jurisdiction. Courts of general jurisdiction are so called that because they have all the powers that a court may have. In other words, there are no limits placed on the types of cases they can hear, the amount of money they can award, or their right to issue injunctions.

In the vast majority of states, the court of general jurisdiction is called the Circuit Court. This goes back to the time in the early 1800s when judges, lawyers, and the court personnel literally rode the circuit. Those who have read Sandberg's biography of Abraham Lincoln will remember long discussions about "riding the circuit." What occurred was that lawyers, court personnel, and the judge would travel as a group to a county seat and decide all the cases that had arisen in that county since the court was last held there. Then they would move to the next county

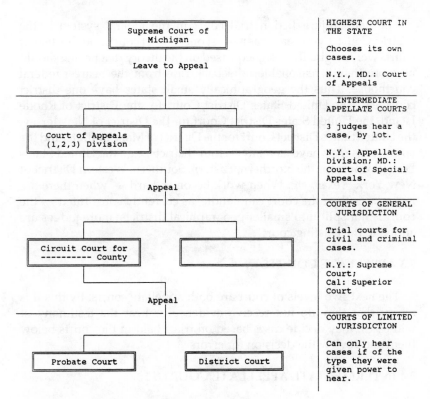

Figure 2.2 State courts (illustrated by Michigan).

on the circuit and hold court there, etc.; and they would cover all the counties in a circuit in a certain amount of time. Thus this is the general jurisdiction court name in the vast majority of states.

Some states are different. As noted in Figure 2.2, in New York the court of general jurisdiction is called the *Supreme Court*. The origin of this name is lost some place in the midst of early New York history, but it does describe one thing — if a lawyer should ever say you can or cannot do something and the Supreme Court of New York has issued an opinion saying you can or cannot do it, you should get another opinion (unless you are discussing New York law, of course). After all, the Supreme Court of New York, despite its name, is merely a general-jurisdiction trial court.

Readers who used to watch "Dragnet" will all remember that, just before the last commercial, they used to say "Trial was held in Division 186 of the Superior Court of the State of California, in and for the County of Los Angeles. In a moment, the results of that trial." This is a certain indication that the general-jurisdiction trial court in California is, as indicated in Figure 2.2, the Superior Court. In most states, however, this level of court is, as stated earlier, called the Circuit Court.

The general-jurisdiction trial court in the federal system is the District Court. Every state has at least one district court, and the district courts were originally designed based on the theory that no one should be more than a reasonable horseback ride from the nearest federal courthouse. Thus the geographically small states have one district court, e.g., the United States District Court for the District of Rhode Island, the United States District Court for the District of New Jersey, the United States District Court for the District of Maryland, etc, and the large states may have as many as four districts, e.g., the United States District Court for the Northern, Eastern, Southern, Western District of New York, Texas, etc. When work becomes hard — when there are more cases than the court can handle, as currently constituted — the court is not split into smaller geographical districts; more judges are added to the existing court.

2.3 APPELLATE COURTS

The next two levels of court are both appellate courts. By this it is meant that they do not receive evidence or hear the testimony of witnesses; they decide cases based on trials held in the courts below them and review the decision for errors.

2.4 INTERMEDIATE APPELLATE COURTS

The third level up from the bottom of the system is the Intermediate Appellate Court. This is the level of court that sits between the trial court and the highest court of a jurisdiction. In the federal system these are called the United States Courts of Appeals, or, in shorthand, the Circuit Courts. See Table 2.1 for a list of the United States Circuit Courts. The Circuit Courts are geographically arranged and hear appeals from all of the district courts within their geographical area.

Being geographically arranged, the courts have, over time, developed different personalities. As a shorthand manner of speaking, lawyers sometimes refer to the Second, District of Columbia, and Seventh Circuits (New York, Washington, D.C., and Chicago) as "liberal" and the Eleventh, Fifth, Ninth, and Tenth Circuits (Atlanta, New Orleans, San Francisco, and Denver) as "conservative." These labels, obviously, do not have universal application and do not necessarily forecast the results of a given case in any given circuit. They are merely a lawyer's shorthand way of saying that in certain types of cases the court will tend to go a certain way. For example, a "liberal" circuit in an environmental case would be more likely to find for the Sierra Club against the government and more likely to find for the government against industry; a "conservative" circuit would be more likely to find

Table 2.1 U.S. Courts of Appeals (by Circuit, n-s, e-w)

First (Boston, 6 judges)
Maine, New Hampshire, Massachusetts, Rhode Island, Puerto Rico

Second (New York City, 13 judges)
Vermont, Connecticut, New York

Third (Philadelphia, 12 judges)
New Jersey, Pennsylvania, Delaware, Virgin Islands

Fourth (Richmond, 11 judges)
Maryland, Virginia, North Carolina, South Carolina, West Virginia

District of Columbia (D.C., 12 judges)
District of Columbia

Eleventh (Atlanta, 12 judges)
Georgia, Florida, Alabama

Sixth (Cincinnati, 15 judges)
Michigan, Ohio, Kentucky, Tennessee

Fifth (New Orleans, 16 judges)
Mississippi, Louisiana, Texas, Canal Zone

Seventh (Chicago, 11 judges)
Indiana, Wisconsin, Illinois

Eighth (St. Louis, 10 judges)
Minnesota, Iowa, Missouri, Arkansas, North Dakota, South Dakota,
Nebraska

Tenth (Denver, 10 judges)
Kansas, Oklahoma, Wyoming, Colorado, New Mexico, Utah

Ninth (San Francisco, 28 judges)
Montana, Idaho, Nevada, Arizona, Washington, Oregon, California,
Alaska, Hawaii, Guam

Federal (D.C., 12 judges)
Nationwide in special types of cases such as patents, copyrights, taxes,
international trade, etc.

for industry against the government and for the government against the Sierra Club.

Most of the states also have an intermediate appellate court. As can be seen from Figure 2.2, there are really very few choices of names: Court of Appeals, Court of Special Appeals, Appellate Division, etc.; in all of these cases the name clearly has the word *appeal* in it to make it plain what the function of the court is. In some states these intermediate appellate courts, being geographically based, also have a tendency to develop a personality type, although the tendency is not nearly as strong as in the federal system.

Almost all states follow the federal system with regard to the manner in which the intermediate appellate courts function. The court will have at least four judges (the numbers for the federal Circuit Courts are given in Table 2.1), but only three of the judges serve as the "panel" to hear a particular case. To avoid the possibility of the lawyer writing an "emotional" brief to appeal to a specific judge, moreover, the judges are assigned to cases on a random basis after the briefs are filed.

If a lawyer believes that a decision rendered by the panel in his or her case is not consistent with previous decisions by different panels of the same court the lawyer can request that the entire court rehear the case *en banc*. This is done by filing a motion for a rehearing en banc. If such a motion is granted, the original panel's decision is disregarded and all of the judges (that is, the meaning of *en banc*) will now hear new arguments and render a new decision. In this way the intermediate appellate courts manage to keep their decisions internally consistent.

The general rule in both the state and federal intermediate appellate courts is that one has the right to appeal to them (if he or she can afford the filing fees and costs). One of the attributes of "due process of law" is the right to an appeal of an adverse decision of a trial court. This was the main impetus to the creation of intermediate appellate courts — to avoid swamping the highest court of the jurisdiction with appeals that were really not worth devoting time to.

2.5 THE ULTIMATE AUTHORITIES

In the federal system, of course, the highest court is the Supreme Court of the United States. The Supreme Court has nine justices and all of them hear any given case. There is a very, very limited right (for all practical purposes, there is none) to appeal to the Supreme Court. The only really practical way to get a case before the U.S. Supreme Court is by the writ of *certiorari*.

The writ of *certiorari* is merely the name for the papers that a lawyer files when requesting the Supreme Court to hear a case. When a lawyer files and asks the Supreme Court to hear a case, his or her job is to persuade the Court as to why the issue involved in the case is important, not why the court below decided the case incorrectly. The point is that the U.S. Supreme Court has a limited amount of time at its disposal, and it is necessary to persuade the justices to spend time on any particular case. The rule for granting *certiorari* is that it takes the affirmative vote of four (one less than a majority) of the justices to grant it and to decide that the Court will hear the case. The theory is that if four of the nine justices believe that it is an important enough issue that the Court should spend time on it, then the Court will spend time on it.

Taking a case to the U.S. Supreme Court, then, is a two-stage process. First briefs are submitted in support of and against the granting of the writ of *certiorari*. These argue why the issue involved in the case is important. If *certiorari* is granted, a second set of briefs is then filed arguing why the decision being appealed should be reversed or affirmed. Most lawyers will go through their entire professional life without ever arguing a case before the Supreme Court. I, for example, have filed two petitions for *certioraro*, but neither was granted.

In most states the same sort of system works with regard to having the case reviewed by the highest state court. In Michigan it is called *application for leave to appeal*; other states may call it by different names, but the basic theory is the same. The lawyer has to persuade the highest court that the issue involved in the case is important enough that it should spend time looking at it before he or she can attempt to persuade the court of the correctness of the result.

What, then, might constitute an issue that is important enough to persuade a high court to look at it? Probably the best argument a lawyer can make to get a case before the highest court is to convince the Court that there is a "conflict among the circuits." By this it is meant that different intermediate appellate courts (Circuit Courts in the federal system) have decided the same issue in different ways. Remember what was said earlier about intermediate appellate courts developing individual "personalities." This can mean that the same federal statute might result in one thing in New York and something else on the other side of the Hudson River in New Jersey, because New York is in the Second Circuit and New Jersey is in the Third Circuit. In fact, there is currently (1989) a conflict among the circuits regarding a major environmental statute, and it has existed for 17 years. The issue is how, on what grounds, and by whom is a decision regarding the existence of wetlands and permits for filling or dredging them decided. Thus this section of the Clean Water Act (section 404) means one thing in Michigan (in the Sixth Circuit) and something else across the state line in Indiana (in the Seventh Circuit). Despite this conflict among the circuits, however, the Supreme Court has not yet granted *certiorari* on the issue.

2.6 FEDERAL JURISDICTION

Since the state and federal court systems look so similar in their general four-tiered structures, what decides whether a particular case ends up in state court or federal court?

Certain types of cases must, under the Constitution, go to federal court. These are very special cases, for example, those involving ambassadors of foreign countries, suits between two states, etc. In the vast majority of cases, however, there are only two bases for federal jurisdiction. These are called *federal question* and *diversity* jurisdiction.

Federal question jurisdiction exists, i.e., the case will or can be decided by a federal court when (1) the case arises under the Constitution, laws, or treaties of the United States and (2) the amount of money involved is greater than $10,000. In order to arise under the federal Constitution, a treaty, or a statute, the Constitution, treaty, or statute must be directly and immediately involved, and its necessity must be asserted by the person who files the law suit; the fact that it might be a defense to the law suit does not confer federal jurisdiction.

Diversity jurisdiction occurs when the suit is (1) between citizens of different states and (2) the amount in controversy exceeds $50,000. None of the parties on one side (plaintiffs or defendants) can have the same state of citizenship as any of the parties on the other side. Also, the suit must be filed in the state of citizenship of one of the defendants. This is due to the historical origin of this form of federal jurisdiction, which was to prevent out-of-state plaintiffs being discriminated against by in-state judges.

A corporation, for diversity jurisdiction purposes, is regarded as being a citizen of two states. It is a citizen of the state in which it is incorporated, and it is also a citizen of the state in which it has its principal place of business. These two states are very frequently not the same; a large number of U.S. corporations are incorporated in either Delaware or New Jersey, even though their principal places of business are not in those states. A look at the stock certificates for the Standard Oil Company of California, for example, reads "The Standard Oil Company of California, a Delaware Corporation."

Some corporations, in fact, end up having three states of citizenship. An excellent example is General Motors. It is incorporated in Delaware. United States District Courts in New York have held that General Motors has its principal place of business in New York — large corporate offices, a major building at the corner of 59th Street and 5th Avenue, etc. The United States District Courts in Michigan, however, have also held that General Motors has its principal place of business in Michigan — again, a large corporate building in Detroit and a very large number of plants manufacturing automobiles. Thus there are three states in which General Motors cannot sue in federal court on the basis of diversity of citizenship: Delaware, New York, and Michigan.

If a case that could have been filed in federal court is originally filed in a state court, it is possible for the defendant to "remove" the case from state court to federal court. In all other instances, however, cases are heard in state courts. In some sense, it can be said that the federal courts are courts of limited jurisdiction, since they can only hear certain specific types of cases, but we do not designate them as such because, no matter what sort of case is involved, they can still decide it.

2.7 LAW AND EQUITY

Having now managed to decide what court a case will end up in, we face the question of what sort of decision the court can give. Fundamentally, decisions come in two types: decisions of law and decisions of equity.

The distinction between law and equity is an historical one, traceable back to medieval England. Criminal cases or cases involving money judgments were handled by the King's Courts, and issues of right and wrong and orders to individuals forcing them to do or not do things were handled by Ecclesiastical (church) Courts. After the Reformation in England under Henry VIII, when the King became head of both church and state, the King's Courts saw no reason why they should give any power to Ecclesiastical Courts. The constant fights between the two sets of courts over which powers each of them had resulted in our modern system, in which "law" and "equity" have been merged into our current general jurisdiction courts, but lawyers still refer to *cases at law* and *cases in equity*.

Cases at law are what we normally think of as law suits. These are criminal cases and cases in which somebody is seeking an award of money for some reason. *Cases in equity* are a little more difficult to understand; these are the cases in which an injunction is being requested. An injunction is an order to a person or organization directing him, her, or it to do or to not do a particular thing. These orders are, obviously, not self-enforcing, but if one disobeys such an order, one is in contempt of court and can be put in jail for an indefinite period of time until one is willing to comply with the court order.

3

The Common Law (Anglo-Saxon) System of Law

The Common Law or Anglo-Saxon legal tradition is based on the laws of England. It is one of the two major worldwide legal systems, the other being the so-called Civil Law or Continental system, which is discussed later in this chapter. The Common Law system is followed in every place in the world that was once a British or U.S. colony or possession — from Antigua and Australia to Zambia and Zimbabwe. There are two principles that are fundamental to the common law system — *stare decisis* and *res judicata*.

3.1 *STARE DECISIS* — FOLLOWING THE PRECEDENTS

Stare decisis means that cases that are similar should be decided in the same way and that it is important to be able to predict what decision a court will render in a given case. This is why the law libraries in a Common Law country are filled with enormous numbers of shelves of court decisions in order to enable lawyers to attempt to find cases similar to the one that they are currently involved in.

The basic argument for *stare decisis* was stated very succinctly by Mr. Justice Brandeis when he said, "It is more important that the ... law be settled than that it be settled right."[1] By this he meant that it is more important that we know what the result will be in a given fact situation than that the result be fair, equitable, or just. It is important that people know that if certain words are included in a contract, they will be interpreted, consistently, in a certain way. If people negotiating a contract do not like the result that would follow from that interpretation, they are always free to use different words; nevertheless, they know that if they use the first set of words the legal result is known.

The classic aphorism arguing against *stare decisis* was written by Mr. Justice Holmes when he said, "It is revolting to have no better reason for a rule of law than that so it was laid down in the time of Henry IV."[2] This, of course, is the argument against what is frequently referred to as "the dead hand of the law." And make no mistake about it, there are many things in law that are the way they are simply because they were, indeed, so laid down in the time of Henry IV (or even earlier). For example, the attestation clause at the end of a will reads the way it does because it was decided, during the 14th century, that if a will had such a clause at the end of it, it was presumptively valid.

As a result of the principle of *stare decisis*, what a lawyer is doing when doing legal research is attempting to find cases that were previously decided that went in his favor and are very close in facts to the case he or she is currently involved in. In the real world, of course, no two fact situations are ever identical. One of the classic stories told to first-year law students to emphasize this point runs something as follows.

*   In the 19th century one of the major types of litigation involved farmers suing railroads for the death of cattle. (This is why locomotives had "cow catchers" on them.) In this story, the plaintiff farmer files suit and alleges that the 11:45 p.m. train out of town ran over his cow and killed it. The lawyer for the farmer does his research and finds out that two years earlier another cow had been killed by the 11:45 p.m. train out of town only 20 feet from the place where his client's cow was killed. Thus he goes into court and argues to the judge that the decision in the previous case, in which the railroad was required to pay the farmer for the cow, is the precedent that is applicable to the current case. The other lawyer, when asked his arguments, gets up and says something along the lines of "Your honor, I beg to differ with my worthy brother. The cow in the case that he is discussing was white, and the cow in our case is brown." Thus what lawyers are always seeking is a "brown cow" case. Despite all the arguments lawyers may make to the contrary, then, it should be apparent that legal reasoning, at least in practice, is by analogy, not by deductive logic.

3.2 *RES JUDICATA* — "WHEN IT'S OVER, IT'S OVER"

The other fundamental principle of the common law system is *res judicata*. This is a direct translation from the Latin, which reads that the thing (*res*) has been decided (*judicata*). What this means is that once you have been to court and had a trial and all the appeals of that trial have finished, the case is over; a suit cannot be filed again for the same reason. This is true even if the law changes after the suit is decided. If a suit is decided and all appeals concluded on December 30, 1988, and the legislature then amends the statute on January 1, 1989, the losing side remains the losing side; the case cannot be reopened. The same is true if the change of law comes about by court decision instead of legislative change.

Res judicata is there to make sure that things do not drag on indefinitely, and, again, as in the case of *stare decisis*, to guarantee that legal decisions have some degree of finality and predictability.

3.3 THE CIVIL LAW OR CONTINENTAL SYSTEM

The other major western legal system, as already mentioned, is the Civil Law system. It is called this because it directly descends from the civil law (as distinct from the criminal law) of the Roman Empire as preserved in the Institutes of Justinian. It is basically the law that is followed everywhere on the continent of Europe and all places that were ever colonies or possessions of a country on the continent of Europe. It is also the system followed in China, which, after the 1911 revolution, imported a team of German scholars to completely revise its legal system.

The basic form of Civil Law that is currently enforced throughout the world descends directly from the Code Napoleon. Although it is called the Code Napoleon, it was not really written by Napoleon; it was merely promulgated during his reign — its origins go back to the earlier period of the French Revolution. Legal historians, being relatively provincial in their outlook, sometimes argue that the most important result of the Napoleonic wars was the spread of the Code Napoleon to all of the countries that Napoleon conquered from Spain to Russia. This is what caused the laws of Europe to be relatively similar.

The fundamental difference between the Common Law and the Civil Law systems is the lack of *stare decisis* in Civil Law systems. There is nothing, in theory, to prevent a judge in a Civil Law country from deciding a case one way today and deciding a virtually identical case a different way tomorrow. The Civil Law system does, however, follow *res judicata*.

This difference has one major consequence. In Common Law countries the legislature passes relatively generalized statutes and leaves it to the courts to figure out how they will be applied in differing fact situations. (Of course, when faced with a statute of a thousand pages, such as the Internal Revenue Code, it is hard to believe that this is a relatively general statute; nevertheless, it is.) In a Civil Law country, on the other hand, the legislature and the executive (through *decrees, orders,* or what ever term is used in a given country) attempts to anticipate, in advance, every conceivable fact situation that might arise and then tell the courts what results should be reached under each of these fact situations. Since it is humanly impossible to anticipate all the fact situations that might arise, the result is that in a Civil Law country, instead of having pages and pages, and volumes and volumes, and shelves and shelves of decided cases to examine, a lawyer has an equal number of pages, volumes, and shelves of statutes and decrees to examine.

On another level, there is a philosophical difference between the two systems. In a Common Law country the general rule is that if there is no statute and there is no common law prohibiting a certain act then the act is permissible. In Civil Law countries the presumption is the opposite; if there is no statute allowing something then it is prohibited. This distinction is particularly appropriate in the area of criminal law, and we shall now briefly examine some of the aspects of Common Law criminal law.

3.4 *MALUM IN SE* — INHERENT EVILS

The basic definition of a crime at common law (as distinct from a crime created by statute, which we shall look at in a minute) is that people cannot do things that are evil in themselves (which is the direct translation of *malum in se*). By this is meant that there are certain things that one knows one should not do, and if one does them one will be punished. In essence, this means that one should not kill, one should not steal, one should not commit adultery; in other words, one should obey the Ten Commandments.

To illustrate how a common law crime can be defined and work, we shall use the case of burglary. Burglary is defined as "Breaking and entering the dwelling house of another at night with intent to commit a felony therein." Each of the four major phrases of this definition has been through centuries of court interpretation, and we now have exact criteria as to what they mean.

Breaking and entering. Picture a structure with a closed, locked, and barred door. If someone takes an ax and bashes down the door and goes in, there seems to be little doubt that the person is "breaking and entering." Suppose that the door is shut and locked, and the person picks a lock and enters; suppose the door is shut but not locked and the person merely turns the knob, pushes, and enters; suppose the door is neither locked nor latched, and the person simply pushes it open; suppose the door is ajar and the person pushes the door and enters; suppose the door is sufficiently open that the person can squeeze through without touching either the door or the jamb; suppose the door is wide open. Generations of court decisions have told us that if the person can enter the structure without touching any part of it, i.e., if one can just squeeze through without touching either the door or the jamb, then it is not breaking and entering — it is merely entering.

What constitutes a *dwelling house*? Clearly it is a structure in which people reside, but, from a long history of derivation through the common law, it is more than that. Before the last century dwelling houses included much more than simply the structure in which the people lived or slept; it included out-buildings such as stables, kitchens, pantries, and, yes, privies. All of these out-buildings were necessary to enable the structure to function as a dwelling house, and this led to the definition of the *curtilage*, which includes the main structure and such outlying structures as are necessary to enable the main structure to function properly.

This concept of the curtilage of a house is of more than academic or criminal interest. Any reader who has a house with a detached garage has a strong interest in the concept of curtilage; it is this concept that results in a detached garage being covered under a homeowner's insurance policy.

At night. At first sight this phrase might appear self-explanatory, but it is not. Do we mean dawn to dusk or sunrise to sunset. What happens if there is a total solar eclipse? Again, generations of court decisions have told us the answer — if it is "too dark to discern the visage of a person at six paces," then it is night.

With intent to commit a felony therein also seems fairly straightforward. The normal felony we think of in burglary cases, of course, is grand larceny; but breaking and entering, etc. with intent to commit arson, with intent to commit murder, with intent to commit rape, etc. would equally constitute burglary.

Burglary is a crime of "specific intent." By this is meant that the prosecution must prove that the defendant intended to commit a felony after breaking and entering; proof that the defendant had the opportunity to commit a felony is insufficient. A person who breaks in, etc. intending to steal a "trophy sword" worth less than the amount necessary to constitute grand larceny (a felony) as distinct from the petit larceny (a misdemeanor) or a person who drunkenly enters the wrong house and is charged with burglary with intent to commit rape, cannot be convicted of common law burglary.[3]

3.5 *MALUM PROHIBITUM* — PROHIBITED EVILS

All crimes other than those that are *malum in se* are created by statutes and are referred to as *malum prohibitum*. This means that they are wrong not because they are wrong in of themselves, but because they have been prohibited. There is, after all, nothing inherently evil about parking in front of a parking meter without putting money into it; it is only a crime because the legislature has so decreed. The vast majority of crimes, then, are of the *malum prohibitum* type.

This is not to say, of course, that there are no "new" common law crimes. Another case that all first-year law students have to read involves a person who was arrested and charged with making obscene telephone calls. Imagine the horror of the prosecutors when they discovered that, at that time, there was no statute prohibiting the making of obscene telephone calls. They then argued to the court that making obscene telephone calls qualified as a *malum in se* crime. The defendant, they argued, obviously knew that one should not make obscene telephone calls, as he made every effort he could to avoid being caught by the police. The mere fact, ran the argument, that there was no legislation prohibiting the act did not mean that one could not be punished for committing it. This argument was accepted by the courts. Thus we know that, as late as 1955, new common law crimes were still being discovered.[4]

REFERENCES

1.   Quoted in Lewis, *Gideon's Trumpet*, p. 84 (1964).
2.   Ibid, p. 85
3.   *Dedge v. State*, 174 So. 725 (Fla. 1937), Sword; *Simpson v. State*, 87 So. 920 (Fla. 1921), "drunken rape."
4.   *Commonwealth v. Mochan, 110 A. 2d 788 (Pa. Super. 1955).*

PART II

Administrative Law and Judicial Review

As mentioned in Part I, the general rule in the United States is that legislatures pass very general statutes and leave it to other branches of the government to "flesh them out." In the area in which professionals frequently interact with the legal system, the agencies that do this work are the administrative agencies.

Administrative agencies are members of the executive branch of the government. This means that, in the federal system, they report to the President of the United States; in the states, they report to the governor. This does not mean that they report directly to the chief executive of their government. Many administrative agencies report to a member of the cabinet, or to an independent board appointed by the chief executive, with or without the consent of the legislature. In order to regulate the way in which administrative agencies go about interpreting and enforcing statutes in the federal government, Congress passed the Administrative Procedures Act (APA).

The Administrative Procedures Act is found in the statutes, in Title Five of the United States Code, beginning at section 551. In brief, section 551 gives the definitions that apply to all of the rest of the statute. It includes in the definition of *agency* all branches of the federal government except for Congress, the courts, military agencies, and the governments of the territories and possessions.

The APA divides agency actions into two types — rulemaking and adjudication. Commentators generally classify these activities under the more general headings of *quasi-legislative* and *quasi-judicial* actions. Quasi-legislative action involves the actual filling out of the words of a statute and stating the agency's interpretation of it. Quasi-judicial action involves holding hearings for the grant of permits, licenses, etc. Each of these activities is subject to different rules under the APA, and we shall look at them individually. The APA also sets forth criteria for review of agency action by the courts. These sections begin at 701 and run through 706, and we shall also examine them in a separate chapter.

The APA incorporates other provisions regarding agency actions; the two most important of these are the "Freedom of Information Act" (§ 552) and the "Government in the Sunshine Act" (§ 552A). We shall not discuss either of these particular aspects of administrative procedure, as there are entire books devoted to these subjects that can be read by those interested.

4

Quasi-Legislative Activities

As the name implies, quasi-legislative activities of agencies are designed to "flesh out" a statute that has been passed by the Congress. The collected rules that have been issued by agencies are gathered together, organized by subject, and then published in the Code of Federal Regulations (CFR). In reading a statute, then, it is important to go to CFR and see how the agency has decided to implement and interpret any questionable provisions of the statute. A series of decisions by the Supreme Court during the 1980s have indicated that courts give considerable deference to the agency interpretations as published in CFR if there is dispute as to the meaning of a statutory term.[1]

4.1 INFORMAL RULEMAKING — "NOTICE AND COMMENT"

Figure 4.1, which diagrams the process of informal rulemaking, shows that an agency can commence rulemaking at any one of three points. Rulemaking can be started by a petition filed by an outside party, it can be started by the agency itself with the publication of an advance notice of proposed rulemaking (ANPR), or it can be started by the agency itself with the publication of a draft rule. Let us start by examining the two versions by which the agency itself can institute a rulemaking proceeding.

If an agency decides that a rule is needed on a particular topic, but they are not certain what type of rule to adopt, the standard procedure is to use the advance notice of proposed rulemaking. This is done by publishing a notice in the *Federal Register*. The *Federal Register* is a publication of the Government Printing Office that is issued every business day of the year and includes new rules, notices of proposed

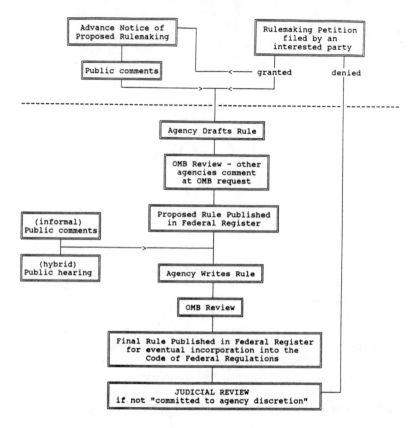

Figure 4.1 Administrative procedures act rulemaking.

rulemakings, draft rules, notices of adjudications, notices of contracts that the government is about to let, etc. In recent years it has been running approximately 20,000 pages per year, but that is very small compared to the size it ran in the late 1970s, when it sometimes got up to 50,000 or more pages per year.

The notice will say that the agency is thinking about writing a rule on a particular subject, and it will request input from anyone who is interested in providing it concerning the nature and content of the rule that the agency should adopt. This applies, obviously, both to new rules and to the possibility of amending or repealing an already existing rule. This method is frequently resorted to by the agency when it wishes to gather information that it otherwise might not be able to get. An excellent example was presented by the EPA's rulemaking proceedings regarding the Toxic Substances Control Act when, in order to get information that industry did not want to release, it published an advance notice of proposed rulemaking, saying that it was thinking of adopting a rule of a type that industry did not believe it could accept.

As a result, industry submitted voluntarily a great deal of information that it would probably not otherwise have given to the agency.[2]

At this point, the two methods of agency-initiated rulemaking became the same. Now the agency proceeds to draft a rule, whether an advance notice of proposed rulemaking was published or not. This will contain, as required by § 553(b) of APA, a draft of the actual language of the rule, a statement of the need for the rule, and a statement of the legal authority under which the rule will be adopted. This entire package is then sent by the agency to the Office of Management and Budget (OMB) for its review. This review by OMB is not required by the Administrative Procedures Act (APA), but it is required by rules issued from the executive office of the President, pursuant to the APA, for rulemaking by all other agencies.

OMB reviews the proposed notice and may request comments from other agencies on the proposed rule, suggest changes, or send it back to the initiating agency. In recent years, however, OMB has, on occasion, had the tendency to kill proposed rules by inaction by just letting them lie on the desk and doing nothing about them. Assuming that the proposed rule and its supporting documentation emerge from OMB, the next step is for the proposed rule and its supporting documentation to be published in the *Federal Register*. This is the "notice" part of "notice and comment." At this point the public and all interested parties submit formal comments to the agency regarding the proposed rule, as provided for in § 553(c). These comments can be of any nature: they can just include legal arguments, they can include arguments regarding the data on which the proposed rule is based, and they can present arguments of efficiency or enforceability regarding the proposed rule. This is the "comment" part of "notice and comment."

At this point in the process, other agencies and the states are treated exactly the same as the general public, and their input is confined to making comments based on the materials published in the *Federal Register*. The *public*, in other words, means every person and organization other than the proposing agency and OMB.

The agency then must take the comments and review them internally before writing a final rule. The courts have held that all substantive points that are raised in public comments submitted to the agency must be discussed by the agency when it writes the final rule. By this it is meant that the agency must say why it has or has not adopted suggestions that are contained in substantively valid comments. As should be obvious, the agency will generate a great deal of internal paperwork at this point in order to decide which comments are important, which are not important, and what to say about them.

After the agency has drafted the final rule in the form it intends it to be issued, OMB again gets a chance to review it. At this point OMB can, if it believes that the rule is not in keeping with the policies of the agency or of the administration, or that it is too expensive (or if OMB has any other objection, for that matter), send the rule back to the agency again. At this time OMB normally does not request input from other agencies regarding the rule; it is reviewing the rule primarily regarding its budgetary and policy impacts.

After receiving clearance from OMB, the final rule is published in the *Federal Register*. In this publication, the agency must also publish its responses to the substantively valid comments it received. All rules published in the *Federal Register* in the course of a year are, at the end of the year, collected and incorporated into the Code of Federal Regulations.

A party who is unhappy with the rule that is finally adopted by the agency (but not another agency) can then appeal to the courts for them to decide whether the rule as adopted should be valid and enforceable. We will discuss how this review occurs in Chapter 6.

4.2 HYBRID RULEMAKING

The "informal" rulemaking discussed above is one of the two varieties of rulemaking that an agency can use, and it is far and away the most common. The other form of rulemaking is the so-called hybrid rulemaking proceeding.

Hybrid rulemaking follows exactly the same sequence of events as does informal rulemaking; however, public comments are not only received in writing, but also at a public hearing, where they may be presented verbally. This occurs when the statute pursuant to which the agency is drafting the rule says something along the lines of "on the record after opportunity for a hearing." Those key words indicate that the agency must engage in hybrid rulemaking.

In a public hearing pursuant to hybrid rulemaking, the provisions of Sections 556 and 557 of APA apply. Thus an administrative law judge or other person must be appointed to preside at the hearing and to keep the record straight. A court stenographer will also be present to transcribe everything that is said by everybody who is present at that time, and all of this becomes part of the rulemaking record.

4.3 EXTERNAL PETITIONS

As can be seen on Figure 4.1 and as mentioned above, there is another route by which rulemaking can be instituted — a petition from an external party. The APA allows individuals to petition an agency and to request it to institute a rulemaking proceeding (for these purposes, of course, rulemaking includes rule amending). This is done by filing a formal paper, entitled a Petition to Initiate Rulemaking, with the agency.

If the agency decides to grant the petition, it can then proceed to either the proposed rule or the advance notice of the proposed rulemaking stage. At this point, the procedures followed are those for informal or hybrid rulemaking, whichever the relevant statute requires. If the agency denies the petition for a rulemaking, the group or person petitioning for the rulemaking proceeding then has the right to appeal directly to a court to determine whether the agency was wrong in refusing to initiate a rulemaking proceeding under the facts presented.

4.4 THE CODE OF FEDERAL REGULATIONS

As mentioned above, the Code of Federal Regulations contains all of the notices that have been published in the *Federal Register*. It is, however, more than just a listing.

It is truly a codification. By this is meant that new rules, as they change old rules, are put into the volume in the amended form instead of in sequential order by date of promulgation. If, for example, some section of the Code of Federal Regulations read "the agency shall, within 90 days, make replies to all requests for licenses that are submitted in the appropriate form," and a new rule amends the 90 days to 60 days, then instead of the Code of Federal Regulations having "90 days," all that will appear is "60 days"; one would not know that it had once been "90 days." Thus, as is obvious, the Code of Federal Regulations is more useful than the *Federal Register*; however, the Code of Federal Regulations always lags one year behind, so after finding out what appears in the Code of Federal Regulations, one must also look at the index to the current *Federal Register* to find out if any of the sections one is interested in have been amended by subsequent publications in the *Federal Register*.

4.5 THE PREFERENCE FOR THE *STATUS QUO*

It should be noted that in any rulemaking proceeding, whether informal or hybrid, there is a presumption in favor of the existing situation. By this we mean that, if there is no rule in place at the moment, then the burden is on the proponent of the rule to show that a rule is needed, and if there is a rule in place the burden is on the proponent of change (whether the change be repeal or amendment). In legal terms this is known as the *burden of persuasion* (see Chapter 11).

In the leading case on this topic the Supreme Court held that the National Highway Traffic Safety Administration (NHTSA) did not have the right to repeal the "passive restraint" (seatbelt/airbag) requirements on new cars simply because it felt that the existing rule was not in accordance with the governmental precepts of the Reagan administration. The NHTSA had to show, the Supreme Court held, that the existing rule would not accomplish the end sought, or that there was some other reason to change the existing requirement.[3]

REFERENCES

1. *Chevron, U.S.A. v. Natural Resources Def. Coun.*, 467 U.S. 837 (1984); *Young v. Community Nutrition Inst.*, 476 U.S. 974 (1986).
2. Bronstein, D. A. and L. S. Wennerberg, "Section 8(b) of the Toxic Substances Control Act: A Case Study of Government Regulation of the Chemical Industry," 13 *Nat. Res. Law.* 704 (1981).
3. *Motor Vehicle Mfrs. Assn. v. State Farm Mut. Auto Ins. Co.*, 463 U.S. 29 (19839).

5

Quasi-Judicial Activities

The other main branch of administrative law is, as mentioned before, quasi-judicial activity, or, as it is normally referred to, adjudication. Adjudication occurs when the statute on which the agency is proceeding requires that the agency grant a permit, license, permission, or other formal activity, "on the record after opportunity for a hearing."

Figure 5.1 shows the sequence of events in Administrative Procedures Act (APA) adjudications. They are normally started by either the person seeking the grant, permit, or license filing an application with the agency; by an outside party seeking a modification of an existing grant, permit, or license; or by the agency itself initiating a proceeding to grant or amend a permit, license, etc. As soon as the petition is filed, a notice of the filing of the petition is published in the *Federal Register*. The *Federal Register* notice has to include the exact nature of the grant, license, or permit sought or sought to be amended; the time and place for filing petitions to intervene or participate; and the timeframe in which the agency expects to conclude the proceeding.

Any person or organization seeking to participate or intervene in the proceeding must then file a notice stating its intention with the agency. The administrative law judge who will preside at the hearing then makes preliminary rulings on the right of the persons or organizations seeking to participate to do so. (One of the major problems frequently encountered in this area is whether the party or organization seeking to intervene has standing. See Chapter 7 for a discussion of standing.) Any party that is granted intervention or participation then proceeds to take part in all further proceedings; parties who are denied intervention or participation have the right to seek immediate judicial review of the ALJ's decision by a court.

The hearing is then convened before the administrative law judge

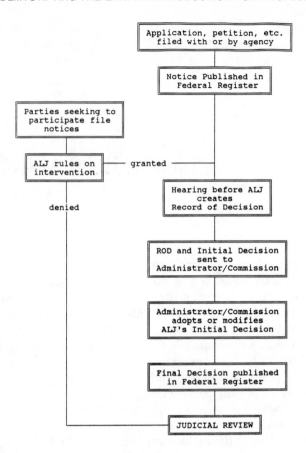

Figure 5.1 Administrative procedures act adjudications.

(ALJ). The ALJ serves not really as a judge, but more as a person who is administering the hearing. The ALJ makes rulings on points of evidence and determines what is admissible into the record, but does not have the power, for example, to put people in jail for contempt. At the hearing before the ALJ, all of the evidence that any party wishes to introduce is ruled upon by the ALJ and, if admitted, made a part of the record. The record will include both evidence and legal arguments regarding the importance and interpretation of that evidence. This whole bundle of materials gathered at the hearing is normally referred to as the *Record of Decision*.

At the hearing things are much less formal than they would be in a court of law. Statements may be presented in writing by the witnesses, they may be presented verbally, or, as frequently happens, the witness presents a detailed statement in writing and then just summarizes it verbally. As a normal rule, witnesses are subject to cross-examination, but the cross-examination is not necessarily conducted by a lawyer. It is not unusual to find experts who are on opposite sides of the issues cross-examining each other, rather than having the lawyers do all the cross-examination.

After the ALJ complies the Record of Decision, the ALJ sits down and, normally, drafts an initial decision. The initial decision is, so to speak, the ALJ's interpretation of the facts and the law as applied to these facts. The initial decision makes a firm recommendation as to what action the agency should eventually take. The initial decision and record of decision are then sent on to the administrator of the agency (or, if the agency is headed by a commission, to the commission). At this point the parties can submit briefs to the administrator or commission arguing in favor of or against the ALJ's initial decision.

If the administrator or commission takes no action on the initial decision of the ALJ within the time specified by statute, then the initial decision becomes the final decision of the administrator or commission. The administrator or commission, however, has the full right to adopt, reject, or modify the ALJ's initial decision.

Whatever action the administrator or commission takes is then published in the *Federal Register* as presenting the final decision of the agency. It is this final decision, as published in the *Federal Register*, that is then subject to judicial review by a court.

5.1 PROFESSIONAL LICENSING AND REGULATION

One of the classic examples of administrative law is the regulation and licensing of the professions by the states. The criteria to be used in the processing of license applications are spelled out by administrative bodies using quasi-legislative methods, and the decision to grant, deny, or revoke the license of any individual is frequently handled in a quasi-judicial manner.

The classic regulated professions are, of course, the so-called learned professions: accounting, engineering, law, and the health disciplines such as medicine, nursing, and pharmacy. The normal structure of the system is to have a part-time commission of some sort that has a full-time staff to handle day-to-day operations. In Michigan, for example, we have an entire department at cabinet level called the Department of Licensing and Regulation, which has 28 boards and commissions who license and regulate various professions and trades. Included are not only the traditional learned professions, but such things as barbers, community planners, hearing aid dealers, land surveyors, morticians, and sanitarians.

An applicant for a license normally has to show appropriate education and training, "good moral character," intent to practice in the state, and, frequently, must pass some sort of examination. Until 1985 most states also required that the applicant be a citizen or, at least, a resident of the state, but the Supreme Court has held such a requirement unconstitutional.[1] Applicants who satisfy these requirements are normally admitted without much dispute on a *pro forma* basis. It is those who fail to meet one of the requirements when applying and those who might, after being licensed, take some action that allegedly demonstrates "unfitness to continue" as a licensed member of the profession who get involved in the quasi-judicial aspects of the process.

An appeal from the denial of a license or an attempt by the licensing authority to revoke a license are normally conducted as quasi-judicial procedures under the appropriate state statute. As a general rule one is entitled to have counsel present, to cross-examine witnesses, etc. It will vary from state to state whether an ALJ-type person conducts it and submits a recommendation for action. In either case, the board or commission makes the final decision, normally by majority vote. That decision, then, is subject to judicial review.

REFERENCE

1.   *Supreme Court of New Hampshire v. Piper*, 470 U.S. 274 (1985).

6

Judicial Review of Administrative Action

Of course, after the administrative agency has acted, a party can take the issue to a court for review by a totally disinterested party. The parts of the Administrative Procedures Act (APA) starting with Section 701 and running through Section 706 detail the ways in which administrative agency actions are reviewed by courts.

Section 701 states that unless a statute "precludes judicial review" or "the agency action is committed to agency discretion by law," the agency action is reviewable by a court. Both of these phrases, of course, are subject to interpretation. A statute that precludes judicial review is fairly obvious; some place in the statute Congress has said something along the lines of "these actions are not reviewable by courts."

What is "committed to agency discretion by law," however, is a more difficult question. It is clear that if the statute says something along the lines of "the agency, in its discretion, may do X, Y, or Z," or "the agency, in its sole discretion, may do X, Y, or Z," then the matter is subject to agency discretion by law. The other major area of agency discretion involves what is called *prosecutorial discretion*.

A prosecutor in the court system always has discretion to proceed with a case, drop it, or settle it. (This, of course, is the basis for "plea bargaining.") In the agency situation, the question arises as to whether the agency can decide not to take action when the statute seems to call for it. For example, if the statute says that the agency shall grant a permit or license on certain facts, whatever the facts may be, and also says something along the lines of "the agency may revoke any license or permit when the licensee or permittee fails to observe the conditions contained therein," is there a requirement that the agency proceed to revoke the license or permit when the condition is violated?

The leading case in this area involved a prisoner on death row who was to be executed by a lethal injection of a prescription drug. He sued to get the Food and Drug Administration to prevent his execution by administration of a lethal dose of a drug on the grounds that such use of the drug violated the license for sale of that drug. It obviously did, since the Food and Drug Administration would never permit a drug to be sold without a label warning what the maximum permissible dosage was. The Food and Drug Administration refused to take any action in the matter. The case got all the way to the Supreme Court, which held that the decision to proceed in this matter was, in terms of APA, "committed to agency discretion by law," as it was a question of prosecutorial discretion. The Supreme Court, therefore, upheld the FDA's decision not to take action in this case.[1]

The APA also says, in section 704, "agency actions made reviewable by statute and final agency action for which there is no other adequate remedy in a court are subject to judicial review." This means that if there is no other solution to your problem with the agency, then you can seek review by a court and, of course, that you can seek review by a court once the agency has taken its final action. Who can do this, however, is a little more complicated. Section 702 says "a person suffering legal wrong ... or adversely affected or aggrieved by agency action ... is entitled to judicial review thereof." This, however, is not a blanket grant of the right to take agencies to court. There are many problems that still exist along the lines of jurisdiction, justiciability, and standing, all of which will be discussed in the next chapter. Assuming, however, for the sake of this discussion, that all of these problems are overcome, the next question is in what court does the review occur.

The very general rule is that reviews of rulemaking proceedings go to U.S. District Court; reviews of adjudications go to Circuit Court. Needless to say, however, a specific statute may overrule this general scheme. For example, EPA rulemakings regarding national ambient air-quality standards are, by the Clean Air Act, reviewable only in the United States Court of Appeals for the District of Columbia Circuit.

Then the next question is, which district court or circuit court? Here the general venue statutes come into play. They generally say that an action can be filed in any court in which the agency has its principal place of business or the person objecting to the agency action has a place of business. Especially in the case of adjudications, which go to Circuit Court, this can result in a mad scramble among the lawyers, which is known as "the courthouse race."

Remember, as discussed before, that different circuits have different personalities ("conservative" or "liberal"). Thus, for example, if I represent a union before the National Labor Relations Board, I would like to get my case into the Second, Seventh, or District of Columbia Circuit; similarly, if I represent management in such a case I would like to get it before the Fifth, Ninth, Tenth, or Eleventh Circuit. The general rule is that whoever files first (in time) gets to choose the court where the case will be heard. This is the "courthouse race."

In some cases, it is truly a race. I can remember a case when I was in practice, 20 years ago, involving the National Labor Relations Board. The case arose in Baltimore, and I represented management. Therefore I wished to get the case reviewed in the U.S. Court of Appeals for the Fourth Circuit, whereas the union wished to get it reviewed in the District of Columbia. The decision was to be handed down at 10:00 a.m., and both the union's lawyer and I were at the NLRB office in Baltimore to receive the decision. At that point, I took the decision, ran down the hall to a pay phone, and, on a line that had been kept open, immediately started talking with a colleague who was in a pay phone in the courthouse in Richmond, the location of the Fourth Circuit.

Each of us had a sheaf of maybe 50 pages, each page containing one paragraph, noting an appeal on one of the issues in the case. I quickly read through the opinion, noting which issues we had lost on and told my colleague at the other end of the phone line "okay, we need pages 1, 10, 15, 17, 22 ... ." He pulled those pages out of his matching sheaf and attached a cover sheet with the name of the parties to those pages and then ran down the hall at his end to the clerk's office to get the papers time stamped. It is the running of lawyers up and down the corridors that is the real "courthouse race". I am sure, however, that this un-seemly behavior no longer occurs and that lawyers have kept up with the advancing technology and now carry portable cellular phones and post themselves right in front of the clerk's desk at both ends, so they no longer have to dash up and down the corridors.

If both parties follow the above procedure and end up with their notices of appeal timed stamped for the same time, what then? The answer, very simply, is that the two courts then arrange, between themselves, to decide which court will hear the case. The normal basis on which they reach this decision is which court has the smaller docket and therefore will get to the case first; this, as a general rule, favors the party that is not seeking review in the District of Columbia.

The case now having gotten before a court, the final question is, on what basis does a court review the agency's decision? Section 706 of APA gives the answers to this question. There are two basic headings under section 706. The court can "compel agency action unlawfully withheld or unreasonably delayed," and it can "hold unlawful and set aside agency actions, findings, and conclusions." The first of these deals with forcing an agency to act when it has not acted. This is less frequent than the second set of criterion, but it most generally occurs in the case of agency denial of a petition to initiate rulemaking.

The second part, holding unlawful and setting aside agency action, contains six subdivisions. The most frequently referenced of these is "arbitrary, capricious, an abuse of discretion, or otherwise not in accordance with law." This is not particularly self-explanatory, because it is very difficult to decide when an agency action is arbitrary, capricious, or an abuse of discretion. There is a huge amount of case law that has tried to interpret what constitutes arbitrary, capricious, or abuse of discretion.

The general statement is that the agency's decision must be "the product of reasoned decisionmaking." This, another verbal phrase, is clearly not much more use than "arbitrary, capricious, or abuse of discretion." How do we determine whether there was "reasoned decisionmaking"? The answer is that a court must engage in reviewing the evidence that was presented to the agency. This review is not designed to decide whether the agency was correct, but to decide whether there was evidence on which the agency could reasonably have reached the conclusion it did. This is the so-called hard look doctrine. One frequently finds reviewing courts saying something along the lines of "although we might not have reached the same decision had we been in the place of the agency, we cannot say that the agency was wrong in the decision it reached." This means that there was sufficient evidence in support of the agency's position that it was not arbitrary or capricious.

The second subdivision of Section 706(2) reads "contrary to constitutional right, power, privilege or immunity." This one is relatively self-explanatory: if the court finds that the agency acted unconstitutionally, then the agency's decision is reversed. The third subdivision says "in excess of statutory jurisdiction, authority, or limitation, or short of statutory right." Again, if the agency has exceeded the limits placed upon it by the statute that created it, then its action clearly cannot stand. "Short of statutory right," however, is a little more complicated. What is meant here is that an agency does not necessarily have the right to grant a limited permit or license when such is requested; the statute may give them the right to grant a permit or license either fully or not grant it at all, but not give them the right to grant a limited permit or license.

The next part of the Section 706(2) says "without observance of procedure required by law." This is a fairly straightforward section, and it means that if the agency fails to take the proper steps (e.g., the agency fails to publish a notice of proposed rulemaking in the *Federal Register*), then a court may reverse the agency decision. It is the subdivision that is frequently involved in delaying or reversing agency action for failure to write an Environmental Impact Statement; if a statement is required and the agency has failed to write one, or has failed to write an adequate one, then a court may find that the agency has acted "without observance of procedure required by law."

The next criterion specified in section 706 reads "unsupported by substantial evidence," but this is limited to cases subject to sections 556 or 557. Sections 556 and 557, as discussed in previous chapters, deal with hearings, and thus apply only to adjudications and hybrid rule-makings. In other words, a court cannot rely on this section of the APA when reviewing an informal rulemaking proceeding. *Substantial evidence* in this subsection means very much the same thing as *arbitrary and capricious* in the first subsection; it does not mean that the court thinks the agency was right, it merely means that the court must find that the agency was not wrong.

The last subsection of 706 of APA says "unwarranted by the facts to the extent that the facts are subject to a review *de novo*." *De novo* means from the beginning; therefore what we are talking about here is that if the court is entitled to retry the matter, i.e., it takes evidence, both documentary and from live witnesses, then a court may decide the case as though it were a regular court case, and it does not have to give deference to the agency's previous findings. This, however, constitutes a very rare occurrence; only in very limited instances of adjudication is the decision of the agency reviewable *de novo* by a court on appeal from the agency.

REFERENCE

1.   *Heckler v. Chaney, 470 U.S. 821 (1985).*

7

Some Technical Hoops and Hurdles

In this chapter we will look at numerous concepts that sometimes impede the ability of people or groups to resort to the courts for resolution of disputes. Some of these are constitutional, some are "judge created," and some are statutory.

7.1 JURISDICTION

According to Article 3 of the Constitution, the judicial power of the United States extends to all "cases and controversies" involving citizens of different states, federal questions, etc. This is the constitutional requirement of jurisdiction. In order for a federal court to hear a case there must be an active "case or controversy."

This means that there must be two sides to the dispute, that the sides must disagree on the issues involved, and that the decision that the court will render will actually resolve the controversy. As early as the 1790s the Supreme Court held that it did not have the power to render what are called *advisory opinions* to the President or the Congress. Advisory opinions are opinions written by a court at the request of another branch of the government giving the court's opinion as to the meaning or interpretation, validity, etc. of a statute. Many state courts have the right to issue advisory opinions upon request but, as noted, the Supreme Court has held that federal courts do not have this power because there is no case or controversy, as there is only one side.

7.2 JUSTICIABILITY

Justiciability refers to the type of decision and subject matter involved in a case. A case is said to be justiciable if it is the type of issue that a court

41

is capable of resolving. The general test used to decide whether a case is justiciable or not is whether it is a "political question." Cases that involve political questions are said to be nonjusticiable, because courts are not political bodies, they are courts.

A classic example of a nonjusticiable question was presented by a case brought by various members of Congress and others in the 1970s to have the Vietnam War declared unconstitutional on the grounds that Congress had never declared war. The plaintiffs in that case wished to have the courts decide that it was impermissible for the federal government to spend any money on the continuing hostilities in Vietnam due to the constitutional violation of the failure to declare war. The courts made very short work of this, finding that it was a political question, not a question subject to resolution by the courts.[1]

Of course, a case that is originally thought not to be justiciable may later turn out to be so. Until 1963, for example, the courts had always held that the apportionment of state legislatures was a political, nonjusticiable issue. In 1963, however, the Supreme Court held that it was not a political question; it was a valid constitutional question and the courts had the right to declare the districting of a state legislature to be unconstitutional on the grounds that, in the United States, the general rule was "one man [one person], one vote."[2] Thus an issue that had previously been thought to be nonjusticiable turned out to be justiciable when the Supreme Court changed its mind.

7.3 STANDING

As should be obvious from the above discussion, both jurisdiction and justiciability involve the subject matter at issue in the case. Standing is different; it involves the question of whether the parties who are raising the issues are the appropriate parties.

The basic idea behind standing is to prevent the courts from issuing decisions in which the best arguments are not presented by both sides. Historically, it is an outgrowth of some "self-inflicted injuries" that the Supreme Court sustained during the 19th century. The most famous of these cases was the "Dred Scott case," which was clearly a "trumped-up" case in that the two parties present before the Supreme Court were really in agreement on the outcome they desired. The less famous but perhaps more significant of these cases was decided in 1895 and held that the federal income tax, which had been passed over 30 years before, was unconstitutional.[3] While subsequent Supreme Courts have never directly criticized their predecessors for deciding such cases, starting in the 1930s the Supreme Court began incorporating provisions regarding standing into its decisions.

The basic issue to be decided in a standing question is whether the party whose standing is questioned has a "sufficient personal stake in the outcome of the controversy" to ensure that the best arguments will be presented. The problem is to determine whether a party has a sufficient personal stake. In 1970 the Supreme Court, in one of its standing decisions, wrote "generalizations about standing to sue are largely worthless."[4] Although almost 20 years have since passed, it is my firm belief that the same statement is still true. To me, as to many other commentators, the following dialogue from Lewis Carroll clearly typifies the problems of determining the differences among many of the standing cases the Supreme Court has decided:

- "I see nobody on the road," said Alice.
- "I wish I had such eyes," the king remarked in a fretful
  tone. "To be able to see nobody! and at that distance too!"[5]

Thus rather than attempt to trace the law of standing to its present position, or attempt to describe it in detail, we will attempt here only to give a general description of the criteria that courts use in determining whether a party has standing.

For practical purposes, standing is divided into two parts: constitutional and prudential. The constitutional standing requirements must be met in order for a case to go forward; the prudential requirements may or may not be applied depending, in my view, on the whim of the court. The current rule for constitutional standing has three parts. First the party must allege that he, she, or it is personally injured or threatened with injury by the challenged action. Two, the personal injury or threatened injury must be traceable to the allegedly unlawful conduct taken by the other side. Three, the party is likely to have its problem resolved by an appropriate decision and order of the court.

Prudential considerations include the following: (1) a party may not assert the rights of other persons or entities who are not parties to the current case; (2) the party must be within "the zone of interest protected by the statute at issue"; (3) a party may not present a "generalized grievance," one in which the party bringing the action has no more stake than any other member of the public; and (4) the party must not be challenging a statute as unconstitutional when applied to another person or entity.

I once wrote a law review article in which I attempted to explain the U.S. law of standing to Australian lawyers. At the end of that discussion I said, "if Australian readers feel somewhat confused at this point concerning the law of standing in the United States, they should not be too disheartened; there is a general belief in the United States, which I share, that the Supreme Court does not really understand the concept either."[6] Therefore if you as a reader of this book are still confused about what standing is and how it is applied, I give you the same advice: do not be too disheartened.

7.4 RIGHT OF ACTION

The next legal technicality that must be confronted by a party seeking to file suit is whether that party has a right of action. What this means is that the party filing suit must demonstrate that it is within the class of people for whose benefit the statute was enacted, and that the statute, as enacted, either expressly grants or implies the right to resort to the courts for its enforcement.

The Supreme Court has said that "whether the petitioner has asserted a cause of action depends not on the quality or extent of [the] injury but on whether the class of litigants of which petitioner is a member may use the courts to enforce the right at issue."[7] In the vast majority of cases this is no major problem, as the statute will, frequently, expressly state that parties may resort to the courts for its enforcement, and, of course, actions filed pursuant to judicial review under the Administrative Procedures Act have a right of action under section 702 thereof.

Assuming no explicit grant of a right of action, there is a multipart test to determine whether there is an implied right of action. The first portion of the test is to determine whether "the plaintiff is one of the class for whose especial benefit the statute was enacted."[8] To satisfy this test, the plaintiff must demonstrate that the statute was passed with the class to which the plaintiff belongs as a specifically intended beneficiary of the statutory scheme. The second part of the test is whether there is "any indication of legislative intent ... either to create a remedy or to deny one."[9] This is really a very hard test to satisfy, because if the statute fails to grant an explicit right of action, and also fails to deny one, it is very difficult to determine what the legislative intent was on this subject.

The third part of the test is to determine whether it would be "consistent with the underlying statutory purpose of the legislative scheme to imply ... a remedy."[10] This test, in effect, asks the court to analyze the entire statute and to determine whether it is a statute of a type that is reasonably suitable for enforcement by private parties. The fourth part of the test is to decide whether the issue is "one traditionally relegated to state law ... so that it would be inappropriate to infer a cause of action based on federal law."[11] This is generally a much easier question to answer. If the suit to be filed is of a standard type, i.e., tort, contract, etc., then it is most likely to belong in state court, not in federal court. If, on the other hand, what is being sought is an injunction against some sort of federal agency, then it will, in all probably, belong in federal court.

In many federal statutes there are special limitations upon the right of action, even though the grant of the right of action is quite explicit. When the issue involved is a citizen suit against an agency, there is frequently a requirement in the statute that the citizen must give the agency notice of intent to file suit before the citizen can actually file the suit. The idea here, obviously, is to put the agency on notice that the citizen believes it has done something wrong and then give the agency a certain amount of time to consider the matter and, perhaps, correct its alleged mistake. In the Clean Air Act, for example, the agency must be given notice and the citizen must then wait 90 days before a suit can be filed; failure to give the written notice and to wait the requisite period is grounds for dismissal.

7.5 RIPENESS

Assuming that a court has found itself to have jurisdiction, that the issue is justiciable, that the parties have standing, and that a right of action exists, the next thing to be determined is whether the case is "ripe" for decision. As the name implies, the Ripeness Doctrine deals with whether this is the appropriate time for a court to intervene in the matter.

Ripeness questions most frequently arise when dealing with federal agency actions. The question is, at what point in the agency action has it become "final enough" that a court can feel free to intervene without getting in the way of the agency's action. The standard test for ripeness is to determine "both the fitness of the issues for judicial decision and the hardship to the parties of withholding court consideration."[12] By this is meant that the court must look at the actual decision that is being sought and determine whether "irrevocable (or, at least, some) harm" would result to either party if the court were to refuse to decide the case at this point.

7.6 SUMMARY

As can be seen from the preceding discussion, there are many technical hoops and hurdles through which a person seeking access to the federal courts must navigate. A relatively recent case may illustrate how these all come together.

In this case the plaintiffs were a neighborhood group who alleged that the defendants, the local planning officials responsible for highway routing in the area, had made a tentative decision to route a major road through their neighborhood, which resulted in a severe diminution of their property values. The neighbors filed suit against the planning body to get a review of the decision in the courts, alleging that the planning body had failed to give sufficient consideration to social, economic, and environmental issues.

The court held that the plaintiffs had standing in this case, because they clearly had suffered injury in fact (diminution of property values), that this diminution of property values was obviously traceable to the recommendation that a major highway be put through the neighborhood, and that an injunction against the planning authority would cause a reevaluation of the property values and thus would rectify the loss. The court further held that there was no doubt that the case was currently ripe for decision, as there would clearly be irreparable continuing injury to the plaintiffs, diminution of market value of their houses, if the court did not act in the manner.

On the other hand, the court held that the plaintiffs had failed to demonstrate that they had a right of action in this type of case. The court held that the Federal Aid Highway Act, pursuant to which the planning body was acting, did not grant an explicit right of review for these preliminary types of decisions; it granted rights of review only once a "corridor" had been officially designated by an agency. Further, the court found that there was no implied right of action in this case, as both the first and second test for implied right of actions failed on these facts. Therefore, the court dismissed the case and held that the plaintiffs, even though they may have been suffering injury, were unable to secure review of that injury in the courts.[13]

REFERENCES

1. *Velvel v. Johnson*, 287 F. Supp. 846 (D. Kan. 1968); Aff'd. sub nom *Velvel v. Nixon*, 415 F. 2d 236 (10 Cir, 1969) cert. den. 396 U.S. 1042 (1970).
2. *Baker v. Carr*, 369 U.S. 186 (1962).
3. *Scott v. Sandford*, 19 How. 393 (1856); *Pollock v. Farmer's Loan & Trust Co.*, 158 U.S. 601 (1895).
4. *Association of Data Processing Serv. Orgs. v. Camp*, 397 U.S. 150 (1970).
5. Carroll, L., *Through the Looking Glass*, M. Gardner, ed. (1960).
6. Bronstein, D. A., "An American Perspective on Australian Conservation Found. Inc. v. Commonwealth of Australia and the Status of Environmental Law in Australia," 13 *Federal L.R.* 76 (Canberra 1982).
7. *Davis v. Passman*, 442 U.S. 228 (1979).
8. *Cort v. Ash*, 422 U.S. 66, 78 (1975).
9. Ibid.
10. Ibid.
11. Ibid.
12. *Abbott Laboratories v. Gardner*, 387 U.S. 136 (1967).
13. *Allandale Neighborhood Assn. v. Austin Transportation Study Policy Adv. Comm.*, 840 F. 2d 258 (5th Cir, 1988).

8

Some Additional Technicalities

After all of the items discussed in the last chapter are considered and satisfied by a party seeking to avail itself of the courts, there are still some other problems that can arise.

8.1 STATUTE OF LIMITATIONS

The first of these is the statute of limitations. The statute of limitations is the time limit within which one must file a suit if one wants to do so. The reason for having a statute of limitations is obvious; it prevents things from dragging on into the indefinite future so that a person cannot suddenly be sued for something that happened 50 years ago. The statutes of limitations normally vary depending on the type of case involved. In a standard civil tort action for personal injuries, for example, the rule is generally two or three years from the date the injury occurred (or the date on which the injury was discovered). For a contract case, it can be anything between one and seven (or perhaps ten) years from the date on which the contract is breached, or the date on which it was executed. For these types of actions, the statute of limitations is set by the legislature by passing a general statute, which says that for actions of type A, the statute of limitations shall be X years; for actions of type B, the statute of limitations shall be Y years, etc.

In the vast majority of cases involving rulemaking by administrative agencies, there is no statute of limitations. This is because those are actions in equity (actions seeking an injunction) and there is no statute of limitations on actions in equity. What there is in equity cases is the doctrine of Laches, which is discussed in Chapter 10.

The most controversial aspect of statutes of limitations at the moment is the *discovery rule*. Under this rule the statute of limitations does not start to run until such time as the party "discovers, or, in the exercise of reasonable diligence, should discover" that there is a potential suit involved in the facts. It is under this doctrine that the long "tail" in malpractice actions arises. If one goes to a physician and the physician misdiagnoses you and continues to treat you based on the misdiagnosis, and you do not realize that there was a misdiagnosis until, maybe four years later, you see a second physician, the discovery rule holds that the three-year statute of limitations would start to run from the time you see the second physician, or from the time a court holds that a "reasonable person" would have consulted a second physician. On the other hand, if the problem is that you went into the hospital to have your right leg operated on and the surgeon operated on the left leg, the statute of limitations would start to run immediately upon your recovery from anaesthesia, when you should reasonably discover that the wrong leg was operated on.

8.2 SOVEREIGN IMMUNITY

The doctrine of sovereign immunity arises from the Common Law tradition that "the sovereign can do no wrong." What this means in U.S. law is that you cannot sue the government unless the government gives consent to be sued, and gives consent to be sued in the court in which you file the suit.

Until 1948, for example, if you were run over by a postal truck while walking down the sidewalk, you could not sue the government to recover for your injuries because of the doctrine of sovereign immunity. The only way that you could recover for your injuries was to have your Congressperson introduce what is called a *private bill* in the Congress and get it passed by both houses and signed by the President, appropriating money to be paid to you for the injury you suffered. Because there were so many such cases, in 1948 Congress passed a general statute providing that anyone who was injured in that type of case (any type of tort case) could sue the government provided that certain preconditions were filled. In other words, the Federal Torts Claims Act created a right of action on behalf of private citizens against the government for torts allegedly committed by the government.

Under the federal statute, this is a limited right of action. Before one can file a suit in federal court under the Federal Tort Claims Act, one must file a claim with the agency and give it the opportunity to pay you out of its own funds, without the necessity of going to court.

In the area of administrative law, the Administrative Procedures Act (APA) was amended in the mid-1970s to eliminate sovereign immunity as a potential defense. Section 702 says that "the United States may be named as a defendant in any such action and a judgment or decree may be entered against the United States." Before that time there had been some cases that had permitted the federal government to raise the defense of sovereign immunity in cases of administrative procedures.

The way that one got around that sovereign immunity defense before the amendment to the APA was to sue not the government, or the agency of the government, but to sue the officer who headed the agency. There is a traditional exception to sovereign immunity, which says that if an officer of the government is acting *ultra vires* then the officer can be sued. *Ultra vires* means beyond the scope of the authority of the individual. Thus it was common to allege that the officer was not doing what the statute required him or her to do, or was doing more than the statute permitted him or her to do, or that the statute itself was invalid because it was unconstitutional. In any of these cases, obviously, the officer would be acting without appropriate authority and thus the defense of sovereign immunity would be unavailable.

Sovereign immunity still applies to actions against state governments, particularly actions against state governments in federal court. The 11th Amendment to the Constitution says that citizens cannot sue a state in federal court without the consent of the state. Virtually no states have given permission for such suits. The only cases in which such permission obviously exists is, as discussed above, those of *ultra vires* action by the state official. Thus if one alleges that a state statute is unconstitutional under the federal Constitution, one does not sue the state; one sues the officer of the state who would be responsible for enforcing the allegedly unconstitutional statute.

Many states, of course, have done the same thing as the federal government and enacted statutes similar to the Federal Tort Claims Act for things occurring inside their state. However, in almost all of these cases, the right to sue occurs only in state court, not in federal court. Thus, even if one is a citizen of another state, which would normally result in "diversity" jurisdiction, one cannot sue a state pursuant to a state tort claims law in federal court. All suits under state tort claims acts are almost uniformly required to go into the state court system.

PART III

Some Specific Legal Issues

In this part we will examine some general and various specific areas of law. Chapters 9 through 14 are primarily concerned with things that happen when a party resorts to the courts to resolve an issue, although Chapter 13 deals with a concept that pervades all of the law. Chapters 15 through 21 present very brief introductions to specific legal topics.

9

Civil Procedure

The rules of civil procedure govern the way trials are prepared for and held in the courts. The standard rules of civil procedure are those used in the federal courts, the Federal Rules of Civil Procedure (FRCP). FRCP was adopted by the Supreme Court in 1938, and most of the states now follow the same general principles in their civil procedure as do the federal courts. Extracts from FRCP can be found in Appendix B. The basic principle of FRCP is what is called *notice pleading*. By this is meant that the papers filed in the courts do not require a great amount of detailed factual information; they merely require enough information to "put the opposing party on notice" of the issues that will be contested at trial.

9.1 COMPLAINT

As can be seen in Appendix B, a trial is commenced by the filing of a complaint. The complaint is composed in numbered paragraphs, each paragraph detailing a different factual allegation. In the federal courts, the first paragraphs of the complaint detail the facts that support federal jurisdiction (either "federal question" or "diversity").

After jurisdictional allegations are out of the way, each allegation is then made in yet another separately numbered paragraph. For example, if we have a simple automobile collision that occurred at an intersection governed by a stop sign, and the plaintiff was on the street that did not have the stop sign and was hit by the car of the defendant, which had the stop sign, the allegations might read something like the following:

1.   On December 5, 1988, at or about 9:00 a.m., the plaintiff was

driving his vehicle westward on 1st Avenue, in the City of Absolute, in the State of Confusion.

2. At or about the same time the defendant was driving his car north on Elm Street.

3. That the defendant approached the intersection of Elm Street and 1st Avenue and failed to stop for the stop sign, which was facing in his direction, as a result of which the cars came into collision in the middle of the intersection.

4. That the collision of vehicles was caused by the defendant's failure to stop for the stop sign, failure to keep a proper lookout for other vehicles on the road, and failure to fulfill the duty to operate a vehicle in a safe and proper manner.

5. As a result of the collision of vehicles, the plaintiff suffered a fractured right humurus, injury to his back and neck, and had and continues to have pain and loss of earnings due to the collision of vehicles and the resulting injuries.

The complaint would then conclude by detailing the relief requested, say, "wherefor the plaintiff prays that defendant be required to pay for plaintiff's vehicle, which was totally destroyed by the collision, pay for plaintiff's medical expenses, and pay for plaintiff's continuing pain and suffering and loss of earnings in the amount of $1,000,000.00." This last paragraph, in a suit seeking money, is referred to as the *ad damnum* clause, and the amount requested is always specified as an extremely large amount. This is done because a court cannot award more than is requested, so lawyers always request the moon to make sure that whatever is awarded is within the *ad damnum* limits.

As can be seen, such a set of paragraphs does not really provide the other party with a great deal of information, but it does serve to give notice as to (1) the cause of the suit, (2) the injuries alleged, and (3) the relief sought.

9.2 ANSWER

When a party is served with a complaint, the proper response is to make an answer. In the answer to the complaint, the defendant normally goes through the allegations of the complaint paragraph by paragraph and either denies them, admits them, or states that the party has insufficient information to either admit or deny. Thus the answer to the above complaint might read that:

1. The allegations of paragraph 1 are admitted.
2. The allegations of paragraph 2 are admitted.
3. The allegations of paragraph 3 are denied.
4. The allegations of paragraph 4 are deined.

5.   Defendant has insufficient information to either admit or deny the
       allegations of paragraph 5.

In this way the defendant would be admitting that the two cars were at
the locations specified, but denies that he was operating his vehicle in
any way improperly and states that he does not know what injuries the
plaintiff sustained.

If the defendant wanted to assert what is called an *affirmative defense*,
the rules would require him to present that in the answer. For example,
if the defendant wanted to argue that the reason the vehicles came into
collision was that the plaintiff's car was going so fast that, even though
the defendant had stopped and looked both ways before entering the
intersection, the defendant's car hit him, then he would have to add a
paragraph to the answer stating something along the lines of:

6.   In addition, defendant alleges that the collision of vehicles oc-
       curred due to the excessive rate of speed at which plaintiff was
       operating his vehicle, and to the plaintiff's failure to maintain a
       proper look out for other vehicles on the road, and to the plaintiff's
       failure to operate his car in a safe and reasonable manner.

Notice that the rules provide that inconsistent allegations may be
contained in an answer. The classic story used to illustrate this for law
students runs something like what follows:

> Mr. Smith filed suit against Mr. Jones alleging that Mr. Jones
> borrowed his black pot and returned it with a large crack in it, and
> seeking money to repair the damaged pot. In his answer Mr. Jones
> alleges several things: that he never borrowed the pot; that he
> borrowed the pot but returned it in good condition; that the pot
> was broken when he borrowed it; that the pot was defective and
> broke in the course of normal use; and that the pot was broken by
> a burglar who entered Mr. Jones' house and ransacked the place.

Under any reasonable interpretation, these defenses are totally inconsistent with each other; nevertheless, it is perfectly permissible
under the rules to file such an answer. Mr. Jones, of course, will have to
choose one of these varying defenses for his main argument before the
case goes to trial.

9.3 COUNTERCLAIMS, CROSS-CLAIMS, THIRD-PARTY
CLAIMS, AND CLASS ACTIONS

Counterclaims are claims made by the defendant against the plaintiff
after the suit is filed and come in two types, compulsory and permissive.

A counterclaim is a claim that the defendant can assert "counter" to the plaintiff's claim against the defendant. A compulsory counterclaim is one that arises out of the same incident, fact situation, or legal situation as the original claim by the plaintiff against the defendant. In our simple automobile collision case, for example, if the original defendant wanted to assert a claim against the original plaintiff for the defendant's personal injuries and the damage to his vehicle, that would be a compulsory counterclaim. A permissive counterclaim, as the name implies, is a counterclaim that is permitted to be, but does not have to be raised in the action. If, for example, the plaintiff in the automobile collision case owed the defendant money based on a loan made previously, that would be a permissive counterclaim for the defendant to assert against the plaintiff.

A cross-claim is a claim made by one party on one side of a case against another party on the same side of the case. Let us, to use an example, assume that a rented small private plane crashes upon takeoff from an airport. The families of the pilot and passengers file suit against everybody they can think of who might possibly be liable: the plane's manufacturer, the company that sold the plane to the owner, the owner of the plane, the company that was responsible for doing the maintenance on the plane, etc. The families of the passengers could then file a cross-claim against the estate of the pilot, alleging that he negligently flew the plane. Similarly, the owner of the plane could file a cross-claim against the company that did the maintenance on the plane, saying that if I am liable for leasing a plane that was in poor condition, it is because you are liable for negligently doing the maintenance and upkeep on the plane. This then would constitute a series of cross-claims among parties who are already in the case.

A third-party claim is a claim by one of the parties in the case against someone who is not currently a party to that case. A third-party claim is handled exactly the same way that an original suit is handled, i.e., the third-party plaintiff must file a complaint against the third-party defendant and have the third-party defendant served with process, etc. Going back to our light plane crash, for example, the manufacturer of the plane, one of the defendants, might decide to file a third-party claim against the manufacturer of the engine and the manufacturer of the propeller, alleging that the engine and the propeller turned out to be unsuitable to the use to which they were to be put, namely, to fly a plane (this is an example of a "products liability" claim). To do this the manufacturer would file a complaint against the manufacturers of the engine and the propeller alleging, in separately numbered paragraphs, the various defects that it believed to be present, and the third-party defendants — the two manufacturers — would have to file answers to the complaint.

The only major difference between this and the filing of a new suit by the manufacturer of the plane against the manufacturer of the engine and propeller is that the case is part of the original suit by the pilot and passengers, not a new and separate case. Once the manufacturers of the engine and propeller became parties to the case, other parties could file claims against them as though they had been original parties. Thus, for example, the estates of the pilot and passengers could make a claim against the manufacturers of the engine and the propeller on the same basis as the claim by the manufacturer of the plane; and the other defendants could also file cross-claims against them. All of this paper filing, and the whole idea of counterclaims, cross-claims, and third-party interpleading is to make sure, to the extent possible, that all potentially involved parties have a chance to present their sides of the case when it eventually gets resolved.

A class action is an action in which many individuals have suffered a certain injury, or have an identical complaint against one or more defendants, and join together to file the suit as one. As Rule 23(a) says, there must be so many people involved that suits by each of them would be impracticable, and there must be a common question of law or fact in all the claims. Thus if there is then a risk of inconsistent or varying adjudications among different parties who are identically situated, a class action can be maintained.

As a matter of actual fact, of course, the members of the class do not normally get together and decide to file suit; what happens is that some individual decides to file suit on behalf of the entire class. This is one of the hallmarks of a class action: the title reads something along the lines of "John Doe, on his own behalf, and on behalf of all other persons similarly situated, versus the XYZ Corporation." That "on his own behalf and on behalf of all others" language is the clear indication that the case is filed as a class action. As Rule 23 also indicates, the plaintiff who files the action must be "representative" of the class, i.e., the injuries of that plaintiff must be similar to those suffered by all the other members of the class.

Once a class action is filed and the court agrees that it is properly filed as a class action, all sorts of requirements come into play to notify the members of the class that such a suit has been filed. Each potential member of the class must be informed in some way (either actually and directly or by publication in a newspaper or similar vehicle) and has the option to continue to participate in the class action or to refuse to participate. Members of the class who refuse to participate are said to have "opted out." If a person who is a member of the class does not opt out of the suit, any judgment that is eventually entered in the case is binding against that party ever filing a similar suit for the same reasons; in other words, it is *res judicata* on the subject. Like counterclaims, cross-claims, and third-party practice, the purpose behind class actions is to consolidate into one place as many of the potential claims arising out of a given problem as possible and to resolve them all at one time.

9.4 DISCOVERY

Since there is so little detailed factual information contained in the initial pleadings, the complaint, and the answer, the rules provide for discovery devices. In the course of discovery, each party seeks to obtain the detailed information on which the opposing party's claim is based. The idea behind this is that "civil trials in the federal courts ... [are not] carried on in the dark."[1] The aim of these liberal discovery rules is to "make a trial less a game of blind man's bluff and more a fair contest with the basic issues and facts disclosed to the fullest practicable extent."[2]

The general provisions regarding discovery are set forth in Rule 26 of FRCP; the next 10 rules after that provide details on each of the possible methods of discovery. (These are not included in Appendix B, as they might well constitute almost an entire book, even for this nonlegal audience.) The general provisions state that the methods of discovery include depositions upon oral examination, depositions upon written questions, interrogatories, requests for admission, requests for production of documents or things, requests for entry upon land, and requests for medical examinations.

As stated in Rule 26, the frequency of use of each of these devices is not limited by rule, but may be limited by a court as a result of a "discovery conference" or of a request for a "protective order." A discovery conference is a meeting, held by the lawyers and the judge, on the record, but not necessarily in the court room, at which they agree on a schedule under which all of the discovery activities will be undertaken. Normally this means that a timetable is set up for taking all of the depositions, for answering interrogatories, for conducting medical examinations, etc., and any objections that might be made by any of the parties are ruled upon by the judge.

If a party believes that he or she is being subjected to "undue burden or expense" or other type of harassment during the conduct of discovery, that party may request a protective order. A protective order is issued by a judge after a full hearing in open court on a motion to grant a protective order. The judge may grant any sort of protective order that the judge believes is suited to the circumstances — from forbidding the discovery completely through no limits at all. A very frequent protective order in many types of cases is a *nondisclosure* order, which says that the discovery may procede, but neither side is allowed to reveal what occurs during the deposition (interrogatories, medical exam, etc.). The most common reason for granting such a protective order is to prevent the disclosure of trade secrets.

Also notice that, under Rule 26, a party who has already responded to a discovery request is under an obligation to supplement or amend the answer given if the party discovers that the original answer was incorrect when made, or, if it was correct when made, that additional information, change of circumstances, etc. has changed the situation so that the answer is no longer correct.

Through these discovery devices, then, each side learns what facts the other side is going to present into evidence in the attempt to prove its case. In our hypothetical automobile collision pleadings, for example, in response to the discovery request the plaintiff might allege that the police investigation at the scene showed that the plaintiff was not speeding, that there was no evidence that the defendant had tried to stop for the stop sign, and that there was no evidence that the defendant's car was any way improperly maintained. The plaintiff would also, in the course of responding to discovery, give to the defendant copies of medical reports from the plaintiff's doctors detailing the scope and extent of the plaintiff's injuries.

9.5 MOTION PRACTICE BEFORE TRIAL

Almost everything that occurs before the trial of a case comes under the heading of motion practice. By this it is meant that all of these issues are raised by way of motions to the court requesting the court to make rulings of one type or another. A motion is merely a set of papers filed with the court asking the court for a ruling on a specific issue. The view of some modern lawyers appears to be that if one handles a case properly, one will never have to actually try it; the whole matter can be disposed of in motions. In fact, people who, when I was in practice, called themselves *trial lawyers* now tend to call themselves *litigation attorneys*. The difference here is, simply, that these lawyers believe that the trial is not the main thing; the main thing is the entire process of litigation, from the filing of the complaint through and including (if necessary) the trial.

Among the most important motions that can be made in the course of the pretrial actions are motions to dismiss under Rule 12 and motions for summary judgment.

9.5.1 Rule 12(b) Motions

As can be seen in the text of Rule 12(b), there are seven specific things that are subject to motion after the filing of a complaint. The allegation of any of these seven items could result in the entire case being thrown out of court, and therefore an answer would not need to be filed. For this reason, these motions are normally made immediately after the complaint is served on the defendant and before the answer is filed. The most important and frequently used of these is the 12(b)(6) motion: a motion to dismiss because, as a matter of law, the plaintiff is not entitled to win the case.

In deciding a 12(b)(6) motion several things occur. First, the judge must assume that all of the allegations in the plaintiff's complaint are true and that there is evidence to support them. That evidence is not presented at the hearing on the motion; its existence is assumed. What the defendant is saying when filing a 12(b)(6) motion is something along the lines of "we do not care whether you can prove those facts or not; even if you can, as a matter of law, you are not entitled to win the case." The judge then, obviously, must decide what the law on the subject matter involved is. If the judge decides that, even granting all the facts in the complaint to be true, the plaintiff is not entitled to win the case, then the case is dismissed and it is over (except for any appeals that may be taken). If a 12(b)(6) motion is granted, it is considered to be a judgment on the merits, i.e., it serves as *res judicata* on the suit and the plaintiff is barred from relitigating the issue.

9.5.2 Summary Judgment

The other major motion that frequently occurs is the motion for summary judgment. This is a motion that can be supported by evidence. The evidence that supports a motion for summary judgment is that which has been obtained by discovery and filed with the court and affidavits (statements signed by and sworn to in front of a notary public) from individuals involved in the case that lend support to each side's position. What does not occur in a summary judgment hearing is the presentation of evidence through witnesses, etc. In deciding a motion for summary judgment the judge looks at all of the materials that are submitted and decides whether, on the basis of those materials, there is no doubt that one party is entitled to win.

A motion for summary judgment need not relate to the case as a whole; it may relate to only a small part of the case. For example, in our hypothetical automobile collision, the plaintiff might move for summary judgment against the defendant on the defendant's claim that the plaintiff was speeding. In support of this motion would be the police accident investigation report, which shows that there were no skid marks or other indications that the plaintiff was speeding; an affidavit from the plaintiff stating that the plaintiff was not speeding; affidavits from people who were standing on the street and witnessed the collision, who state that the defendant was not speeding, etc. If the defendant fails to present any countervailing evidence, whether in the form of affidavits, testimony from expert "accident reconstruction specialists," or in any other means, then the judge would probably grant summary judgment to the plaintiff on the specific issue of whether the plaintiff was speeding at the time of the collision.

9.5.3 Motion to Substitute Parties

Another type of motion that is sometimes filed before a trial is a motion for substitution of parties. Rule 25 deals with the substitution of parties. The most common case in which this sort of situation arises is when one of the parties dies before the case comes to trial. If, for example, the plaintiff dies and the action survives the death (some actions, e.g., libel, slander, etc., do not survive the death of the plaintiff), the estate of the plaintiff is substituted for the plaintiff as the party to the case; in the same way, if the defendant should die or if a defendant corporation is bought out by another corporation, the estate of the individual or the purchasing corporation, as the case may be, can be substituted as the named defendant. In a suit against a government officer in his official capacity, if the government official leaves his position, the new occupant of the position is substituted for the original party.

9.6 MOTIONS DURING AND AFTER TRIAL

9.6.1 Directed Verdict

During the course of a trial it is very common that one of the parties, particularly the defendant, might make a motion for a directed verdict under Rule 50. The claim presented by such a motion, which is made after the other side has concluded its part of the trial, is that all of the evidence submitted by the other side still is insufficient to permit it to make a recovery. In effect, this is similar to the 12(b)(6) motion that was discussed above, except that there is no longer any assumption that the plaintiff (or defendant) can prove the facts alleged in the complaint or other matter; it is a motion stating that they have failed to prove such matters. Like a motion for summary judgment, a motion for a directed verdict may be made for only part of a case, or for only one or more of the issues involved in the entire case. If a motion for a directed verdict is granted, then the case stops at that point and the matter is considered to have been resolved; it is a decision on the merits and serves as *res judicata.*

9.6.2 Judgment Notwithstanding the Verdict

If a motion for a directed verdict is denied, and the case proceeds to its conclusion after a full trial, and the party who made the motion for the directed verdict loses, that party may, at the end, make a motion for a judgment notwithstanding the verdict under Rule 50 (frequently referred to as judgment N.O.V. for *non obstanto verdicto*). This is a motion that says to the court that the judgment entered by a jury is incorrect as a matter of law and that the court should therefore reverse it. If the court does reverse it, then the decision of the jury is set aside and the case is decided in favor of the party who made the motion for judgement notwithstanding the verdict.

9.6.3 New Trial and Relief from Judgment

Motions for judgment notwithstanding the verdict are normally combined with motions for a new trial. The idea here is that, although the judge may not be willing to totally overrule the jury's verdict, the judge may be willing to grant a new trial based on the assumption, as detailed in Rule 59, that something went wrong in the trial. Normally what is alleged is an error in the admission of evidence, but other grounds are possible. If the motion for a new trial is granted then the case is set to be tried again, from the beginning, before a different jury.

Notice also that under Rule 60 it is possible, within one year after the entry of a judgment, to file a motion for relief from that judgment. It must be admitted, however, that very rarely are such motions granted, especially when filed a considerable time after the conclusion of the trial and entry of the original judgment. The most common grounds for the granting of such a motion are, as detailed in Rule 60(b), newly discovered evidence and fraud upon the court.

REFERENCES

1. *Hickman v. Taylor*, 329 U.S. 495, 501 (1938).
2. *U.S. v. Proctor & Gamble Co.*, 356 U.S. 677, 683 (1958).

10

Special Issues in Equity

All of the matters discussed in the last chapter regarding the rules of civil procedure relate to cases both in law and equity. There are, however, some special considerations that arise when the case is filed as one in equity. Remember from our earlier discussions that by equity courts we mean requests for special, normally injunctive, relief directed against a party, and not for money. Rule 65 of FRCP relates particularly to actions in equity.

10.1 TEMPORARY RESTRAINING ORDERS

If a person who is filing an action in equity believes that he will be severely injured unless the defendant is required to stop whatever it is that the party filing the suit objects to immediately, the party filing the suit seeks a temporary restraining order at the same time that the suit is filed. Rule 65(b) states that, if at all possible, the other side (the potential defendant) should receive some sort of notice about the request for the temporary restraining order. The comments to this rule by the committee that drafted it make it clear that informal notice by telephone is sufficient; a formal notice served by a sheriff or sent by mail might be preferred, but it is not required.

In the request for a temporary restraining order, the party seeking the order must allege and support by affidavit or other manner that he or she will suffer irreparable injury if the order is not issued. A temporary restraining order can be issued for a maximum length of 10 days and can be renewed for another 10 days, making a total of 20 days. The purpose of the temporary restraining order is to freeze everything in *status quo* and thus prevent any changes of position by the parties that might detrimentally affect the relief sought by the plaintiff in the event the plaintiff were to eventually win.

Before a temporary restraining order is issued, the court may require that the person seeking the order post security. This is a sum of money (normally a bond issued by an insurance company) that will be available to the potential defendant in the event that he suffers damages due to the delay in activities imposed by the temporary restraining order. The amount of the security is set by a court in the amount it believes proper to reimburse the defendant in the event that becomes appropriate.

10.2 PRELIMINARY INJUNCTION

The next step in an equity case, whether or not a temporary restraining order has been issued, is that the plaintiff normally seeks a preliminary injunction. A preliminary injunction, like a temporary restraining order, is designed to freeze things as they are until such time as a full trial can be held. Requests for temporary restraining orders take precedence over all other civil cases in the courts except, obviously, for other preliminary injunction cases that are already pending.

The classic analysis of whether a court will issue a preliminary injunction is a four-part test:

1.   Has the plaintiff convinced the court that he or she is likely to succeed after the full trial? This, obviously, is a major part of the decision of the court to issue or not issue a preliminary injunction. If it is unlikely that the plaintiff will win in the long run, then it would not be appropriate to stop the defendant from carrying on whatever activities are planned.

2.   Has the plaintiff shown that he or she will suffer an irreparable injury if the preliminary injunction is not granted? This, normally, is the second most important item that the trial judge must examine. If the defendants were to continue their activities, and thus injure the plaintiffs, but the plaintiffs would have an adequate remedy, i.e., could be compensated by money, then an injunction would probably not be issued. On the other hand, if the injury would be to health or to the environment, for example, then it could not be made good by the payment of money and it would be irreparable injury under this test.

3.   Will the grant of a preliminary injunction cause significant harm to the defendant? If the defendant would not be harmed in the least by the issuance of the injunction then, obviously, it is a lot easier for the court to consider awarding it. If, on the other hand, the defendant would sustain major injury or encounter serious cost or time obstacles, this would weigh against the issuance of the injunction.

4.   What is the equitable solution? This involves the court weighing the potential harm to the plaintiff under subsection 2 of the test against the potential harm to the defendant under subsection 3. Always, however, remember that part 1, the probability of ultimate success on the merits, must have been established before we reach any of the subsequent parts. If the harm to the defendant by the issuance of the injunction is less than the harm to the plaintiff by the failure to issue an injunction, then the injunction will probably be issued, and vice versa.[1]

10.3 INJUNCTION

After a full trial on the merits is eventually held, the court must decide whether or not to issue an injunction. The injunction is the final order in such an equity proceeding, and it directs the defendant to do or not do a specific thing or things for the never-ending future. Injunctions, like other court orders, are not self-enforcing; the written order by a judge does not prevent the defendant from doing something. What it does do is tell that person that if that thing is done he or she can be found in contempt of court for violating the order and fined or put in jail, as the judge might deem most appropriate. Again, as in the case of the preliminary injunction, the fashioning of the remedy to be granted (i.e., the specific terms of the injunction) is subject to a great deal of discretion from the court. The court is expected, when sitting in equity, to "tailor" the remedy to suit the problem that is presented.

10.4 LACHES

One other special item in equity proceedings should be mentioned, the doctrine of laches. There is no such thing as a statute of limitations in equity cases. If wrong is being done it should be corrected, no matter how much time may have elapsed, or at least that was the original thinking in equity actions. In practice, however, the doctrine of laches serves as the equivalent of a statute of limitations.

Under this doctrine, if the court determines that the plaintiff has "slept on its rights," then the court will dismiss the case. Normally this requires more than the mere passage of time; the defendant must have somehow significantly changed its position based on the fact that the plaintiff has done nothing before the time of the filing of the action. If this has occurred then, the reasoning goes, it would be inequitable (unfair) to permit a request for an injunction to go forward if no objection to the action had been made at the time the action was originally contemplated or at the time it was originally effected. The doctrine of laches, thus, serves as the "gatekeeper" to the courts of equity.

REFERENCE

1.   See, e.g., *Sierra Club v. Ruckelshaus*, 344 F. Supp. 253 (D.D.C. 1973).

11

Some Criminal Law Concepts

As we all know, a section of a book of this type devoted to criminal law could go on indefinitely; in fact, it could constitute a whole book in itself. For that reason this chapter will only introduce and discuss briefly a few concepts that cross all types of criminal cases. The first two of these, *mens rea* and *actus reus*, combine to make the frequently misunderstood third concept, *corpus delicti*.

11.1 EVIL MIND

The evil mind, or *mens rea* in Latin, is a necessary part of any criminal prosecution. This does not mean that the person who committed the criminal act or, we should say, allegedly committed the criminal act, has to be an evil person; it merely means that the person intended to commit the act that is the subject of the crime. It is called *evil mind* because of the traditional common law criminal approach under which, as discussed earlier, crimes were things that people knew they should not do and, if they did them it could be said that they had evil minds.

The modern usage of *mens rea*, however, merely implies that the person intended to commit the act that he or she in fact committed. Thus, although there is nothing inherently evil about parking in front of a parking meter without putting money into the machine, if one can establish that the person intended to do that act, then the *mens rea* for criminal conviction of illegal parking would be sustainable.

11.2 EVIL ACT

The evil act, or *actus reus*, is the other fundamental part of a crime that must be established. By this it is meant that the act actually occurred.

Again, it is called an "evil" act because of the common law derivation of the criminal law. Thus proof that one did indeed park at the parking meter and did not put money into it is sufficient to establish *actus reus*.

11.3 THE BODY OF THE CRIME

Despite anything one may believe based on detective stories in books or on television, the *corpus delicti* has nothing to do with a body of a person who has been a victim of a homicide. *Corpus delicti* translates directly to "body of the crime," and is a technical legal term that means that before a crime can be established and a person convicted of it, both the *mens rea* and the *actus reus*, the evil mind and the evil deed, must be established.

In other words, the *corpus delicti* in a criminal case is nothing more than the basis of the proof that the prosecution must make in order to get a conviction of the defendant.

11.4 SCIENTER

Since the vast majority (or, all) modern criminal law is of the *malum prohibitum* variety, the concept of *scienter* has been developed as a lesser variant upon *mens rea*. To establish *scienter* the prosecution merely has to demonstrate that the defendant knew what act he or she was engaged in and intended to engage in that act; in other words, knowledge and intent. The fact is, however, that not all *malum prohibitum* crimes even require *scienter*.

A classic example of crimes that do not require *scienter* is violating the Migratory Bird Treaty Act. As discussed many chapters ago, the Migratory Bird Treaty Act was enacted pursuant to a treaty entered into between the United States and Canada to regulate the hunting (in the statute, the word *taking* is used) of migratory birds in North America. In one famous case, for example, the defendants were convicted of violating this act by shooting morning doves in a field that had been baited with grain to attract the birds. The defendants contended that they had not placed the bait there and, in fact, did not even know it was there. Despite the government's failure to disprove these contentions of the defendants, however, the court in that case convicted them, finding that neither "guilty knowledge or intent" was necessary in order to convict somebody of violating the Migratory Bird Treaty Act.[1]

In the corporate setting, however, the *scienter* has yet another connotation. In order to convict a corporation of acts committed by its agents or employees, even totally *malum prohibitum* acts such as violating the Migratory Bird Treaty Act, it must be shown by the prosecution that somebody with decisionmaking authority in the corporation knew or should have known that the act would or might be committed.

In a leading case, for example, a corporation that manufactured pesticides had some problems with its equipment, as a result of which pesticides ended up in its on-site sewage treatment lagoon. Being the season when migratory birds migrate, many migratory birds would land in the sewage treatment pond and eventually die from eating things in that pond. The company was prosecuted for violating the Migratory Bird Treaty Act on the grounds that it was "taking" migratory birds. The corporation, in its defense, showed that not only had it not known that the pesticide was in the lagoon, but also that once it discovered the pesticide was there it took all the steps it could to discourage the birds from landing there and feeding, including firing off blank shotgun shells to scare the birds away. Nevertheless, the court held that, since the company was in the business of producing a pesticide that was known to be toxic to birds and animals, it should have known that it was likely that, if a problem arose, some of the chemical might end up in the pond and thus result in the death of migratory birds. On this basis the conviction of the company, as a company, was upheld by an appeals court.[2]

REFERENCES

1.   *U.S. v. Schultze*, 28 F. Supp. 234, 236 (W.D. Ky. 1939).
2.   *U.S. v. FMC Corp.*, 572 F. 2d 902 (2d Cir. 1978).

12

"Burden of Proof"

The title of this chapter is set in quotation marks because, although it is a term that is frequently used by lawyers, judges, and laymen, it is not a term that is favored by academic legal commentators. Those of us who consider ourselves legal scholars perfer to subdivide the phrase into two parts — the burden of persuasion and the burden of going forward with evidence.[1] In this chapter we shall follow the academic tendencies of the author and consider these two items separately.

12.1 BURDEN OF PERSUASION

The reason for the division of "burden of proof" into two parts by academic commentators is very simple: there are two different things happening that are covered by the one term. The most common usage of the term, however, and it is frequently completely unambiguous, is that the burden of proof means the burden of persuasion.

Burden of persuasion means the degree to which the finder of facts must be persuaded by the evidence that the fact is true. There are many different burdens of persuasion, and we shall examine a few of them now.

12.1.1 Beyond a Reasonable Doubt

All readers are, no doubt, familiar with the fact that in a criminal case the prosecution is required to prove that the defendant is guilty beyond a reasonable doubt. This means that if the finder of fact (whether judge or jury) is in any doubt as to whether the defendant is guilty, then it cannot find the defendant guilty because there is a reasonable doubt. If one were to picture the scales of justice, what this means is that one side has to be way down close to the ground while the other side has to be way up in the air; that is beyond a reasonable doubt.

12.1.2 Preponderance of the Evidence

The major burden of persuasion in civil cases is that of a preponderance of the evidence. By this it is meant that before the finder of fact can decide that a given statement is true or a given event occurred, it must find that to be true by a preponderance of the evidence. Again, picturing the scales of justice, they merely have to tip slightly towards the side that is asserting the fact or event; that is a preponderance (more than half).

12.1.3 Clear and Convincing Evidence

Clear and convincing evidence is something more than a preponderance, but still less than beyond a reasonable doubt. Picturing, again, the scales of justice, they should be significantly out of balance, but do need not be overwhelmingly tilted either way. The most common use of this burden of persuasion is in civil cases alleging fraud. The general rule is that civil fraud must be proved by clear and convincing evidence.

12.1.4 Substantial Evidence

Another test for the burden of persuasion that is sometimes used, and that we encountered previously in our discussions of administrative law, is the test of substantial evidence. By this it is meant that if there is substantial evidence, which can be less than a preponderance, then the finder of fact can find in favor of that side. In other words, this is a burden of persuasion that requires not that the fact finder be convinced, but that he or she not be unconvinced that a given event occurred or that a given fact is true.

12.1.5 Who Bears the Burden

As implied in the preceding paragraphs, the burden of persuasion or, as it is sometimes referred to, the risk of nonpersuasion, rests upon the party that is asserting that a given event occurred or that a given fact is true. In the normal criminal case, for example, the burden of persuasion, beyond a reasonable doubt, is on the prosecution to prove the *corpus delicti* and the identity of the defendant. In the normal civil case, the burden of persuasion, preponderance of the evidence, is on the plaintiff to establish that the plaintiff is entitled to the relief asked for in the complaint.

However, this is not always true, especially in the civil case. Think back to the hypothetical automobile collision that we discussed several chapters ago. In that case, when the defendant alleged in his answer to the complaint that the plaintiff was speeding and failed to keep a proper look out, etc., the burden of persuasion on whether or not the plaintiff was speeding would be upon the defendant. This is because the defendant is the party seeking to establish that a given fact is true or a given event occurred.

12.2 BURDEN OF GOING FORWARD

As should be obvious from the above discussion, the burden of persuasion is set at the beginning of the trial based on the pleadings, and it never changes during the course of the trial. The burden of going forward, however, does shift back and forth between the parties.

The burden of going forward is initially on the same person who has the burden of persuasion. It is that party's responsibility to produce some evidence to support its argument that its version of events is correct. Once it has presented enough evidence that a jury or judge could find for that party, then the burden of going forward shifts to the other party. The other party now has the burden of coming forward with evidence to convince the judge or jury that the event did not occur or that the fact is not true.

In most situations the party who has the burden of going forward has the right to just stop and not go forward on any given issue. By this we mean that the fact that one side does not present evidence controverting the other side's evidence does not automatically mean that the first side will lose on that issue; it can still argue that the evidence presented by the other side is weak, is presented by prejudiced witnesses, etc., and therefore should not be believed. It is not incumbent upon an party to go forward merely because the burden has shifted to it.

However, if a party does go forward and present evidence to controvert the evidence presented by the other party, the burden of going forward would now shift, once again, to the first party. That party would now have the obligation of coming forward with whatever evidence it might happen to have, which it had not previously presented, regarding the issue. It is very rare, obviously, that we reach this stage, because it is not generally a good idea not to put all your evidence in at the first opportunity you have, since if the other party does nothing you will not get a second opportunity. Nevertheless, this shifting back of the burden is possible. Indeed, it could shift back and forth again and again, at the discretion of the judge in deciding to admit new evidence on an issue that has already been discussed.

12.3 PRESUMPTIONS

The way in which the law changes the burden of persuasion and/or the burden of going forward is frequently with presumptions. A presumption is exactly that; it is presumed that a given fact is true or that a given type of event occurred as a matter of law. This does not, of course, mean that anybody really believes that the event or fact occurred, but merely that, for legal purposes, we will presume that.

12.3.1 *Res Ipsa Loquiter*

One of the most common burden-shifting presumptions in law is *res ipsa loquiter*, which translates as "the thing speaks for itself." It is generally stated to be something along the lines of, if a party is injured and the injury occurred totally beyond the control of the injured party and the injured party has no evidence as to what occurred and is unable to get any, then it is presumed that the injury was due to the action of the defendant. The classic example of *res ipsa loquiter* would be something along the following lines:

- A person goes into the hospital to have the right foot operated upon. Upon recovering from anaesthesia, the person discovers that the left foot has been operated on. Since the person was rendered totally unconscious due to anaesthesia, there is no way for the person to know what really happened and why the other foot had been operated on. There is an injury, since the wrong foot was operated on and, thus, the presumption of *res ipsa loquiter* will come into play, and it will be up to the hospital, physicians, etc. to both come forward with evidence and, perhaps, to bear the burden of persuasion on why this untoward event occurred.

12.3.2 RPAR

An example of burden shifting presumption from an administrative arena is the *rebuttable presumption against registration* (RPAR) in the pesticide laws, which is referred to as the RPAR process. Under the RPAR process, when the government suspends or cancels a pesticide, a presumption is created that the pesticide is not worthy of being registered. In other words, the burden of going forward and the burden of persuasion shift from the agency to the manufacturer of the pesticide to demonstrate that the pesticide is an appropriate one for use by the public.

The RPAR procedure is poorly named, because there is, really, no such thing as a nonrebuttable presumption; all presumptions are rebuttable, since a presumption is merely a means of shifting the burdens of persuasion and going forward.

REFERENCE

1. See, e.g., Cleary, ed., *McCormick on Evidence*, 3rd ed. (1984), Ch. 36.

13

The Reasonable Person

One of the concepts that runs through all fields of the law is that of the reasonable person. Like the rational person of economic analysis, the reasonable person of legal analysis is entirely fictitious; no such person has ever existed, and none of us would want to know such a person if he or she did exist. The function of the reasonable person is to serve as a standard against which real human actions are measured for legal purposes.

Examples of the use of the reasonable person will be discussed in some of the later chapters involving torts, contracts, etc., but a brief introduction is needed here. Since we will be discussing other examples later, the example that we will use here is one taken from the criminal law.

If, in a prosecution for homicide, the defendant pleads self-defense, the inquiry that must be answered by the jury is whether a reasonable person in the defendant's position would have considered himself or herself to be in imminent danger of receiving severe bodily harm. If the answer to this question is no, then the law says that the defense of self-defense is unavailable; if the answer to this question is yes, then we can proceed to determine what the reasonable person would do facing the reasonable fear of imminent injury.

If the jury concludes that a reasonable person in that position would have acted at least as strongly as did the defendant, then the defense of self-defense has been established. If, on the other hand, the jury should find that the reasonable person faced with the defendant's situation would have taken some less drastic action, then the defense of self-defense has failed.

One of the major problems of using the reasonable person is that we can end up with some very unreasonable results. A classic illustration

77

of this would again be a self-defense situation. If a person could reasonably believe that he or she is about to be attacked by somebody who is 10 times larger and a trained street fighter, but who has no weapon, is it reasonable to shoot the attacker? The traditional legal answer is that no, it is not reasonable to shoot somebody who is attacking you with bare fists, because the response is not commensurate with the threat and the reasonable person never overreacts. The problem with the reasonable person is that it is a person who lacks any emotions; the reasonable person does not know irrational fear; or engage in irrational actions; in fact, the reasonable person is an exceptionally dull, level-headed, unemotional, unexcitable, perfectly calculating individual — a total bore.

There is even a problem inherent in the terminology of the reasonable person. Let us assume that a jury has found a person either guilty or innocent of homicide after a defense of self-defense. (It does not matter which decision the jury made for these purposes.) An appeal is taken to an intermediate appellate court, where the three judges split two to one, two voting to uphold the jury's decision, and one voting to reverse the jury's decision on the grounds that a reasonable person would not have behaved in that manner. We now have a total vote of 1 trial judge, 12 jurors, and 2 appellate judges, 15 people, versus 1 appellate judge on the other side. The case is then appealed to the highest court of the jurisdiction, where the judges vote, three to uphold the lower court decision and four to reverse it.

We now have a situation where there have been a total 18 people deciding that the actions were reasonable, and 5 people deciding that the actions were unreasonable, but the 5, since 4 of them are members of the highest court, manage to tell us that the other 18 are all wrong. In other words, 5 people can decide that the other 18 people are not reasonable persons. There is something wrong with the concept of reasonable person when it can lead to such strange outcomes.

14

Evidentiary Privileges

There are a large number of pieces of relevant evidence that will not be admitted into evidence at a trial and therefore will not be considered by the finder of fact, whether it be a judge or a jury. These are called *privileged materials*, and the general rule is that there is a public policy reason for excluding items of this type from disclosure at a trial. The most common of these privileges are the privileges against self-incrimination, the attorney-client privilege, and the physician-patient privilege. Each of these will be discussed separately in this chapter, and then we will discuss other privileges as well.

14.1 SELF-INCRIMINATION

The most famous of all evidentiary privileges, of course, is the privilege against self-incrimination as stated in the Fifth Amendment to the Constitution. The purpose of the privilege is obvious: to prevent the extortion of confessions from individuals, whether by torture or otherwise. The secondary purpose is to require that the prosecution in a criminal case do its preparatory work properly and conduct a sufficient investigation to be sure that the person they are attempting to convict is, in the opinion of the prosecution, really the perpetrator of the offense.

As we all know from reading the newspapers in the past 20 years or so, there is a way that this testimony can be secured, even though it might expose the testifier to possible incrimination, and that is the grant of immunity. Grants of immunity come in two types: limited and general. A general grant of immunity says that, in return for the testimony to be presented, the government will undertake not to prosecute the person for any crimes that might be disclosed. A limited grant of immunity says that the government will not prosecute the person based on the evidence to be presented in the testimony, but it does not prevent prosecution if the government comes up with independent evidence, not based on the testimony presented by the individual.

The privilege against self-incrimination, of course, is explicitly in the Fifth Amendment applicable only to the federal government. The Fourteenth Amendment, adopted after the Civil War, expands this protection of the federal Constitution to people involved in potential state criminal offenses. The privilege against self-incrimination is one of the mainsprings of U.S. law, and it is the author's opinion that any attempt to weaken it would be contrary to the best interest of the country.

A currently highly debated issue in self-incrimination is whether the privilege is available to corporations, as distinct from individuals. I have argued elsewhere that this privilege should not be available to corporations, and will not repeat those arguments here, but the fact remains that the Supreme Court has held that such a privilege does exist for corporations.[1]

14.2 ATTORNEY-CLIENT PRIVILEGE

The attorney-client privilege is based on the public policy of encouraging people to seek appropriate advice. It is obvious that if the lawyer is not told everything that the lawyer needs to know, then the advice given may not be appropriate. Therefore this privilege encourages clients to tell their lawyers everything so that they can receive appropriate legal advice.

What this does is to put a duty on the attorney to hold confidential any information that is received from the client. This is true of all the nonconstitutional evidentiary privileges; the recipient of the communication is under the duty to preserve confidentiality, while the maker of the communication receives the privilege that is discussed. Like all privileges of this type, of course, there are some exceptions, and there are ways in which the holder of the privilege can waive it.

The main exception to the attorney-client privilege is the *future crime exception*. Under this exception, a communication is not privileged if it divulges the client's intent to commit a crime in the future. The attorney is under an obligation to attempt to dissuade the client from committing the crime, and if the lawyer fails in this duty, the lawyer may have an obligation to report it to the appropriate authorities.

The attorney-client privilege is not created if the communication is not made under conditions that would indicate that it is intended to be kept confidential. The most common instance in which this arises is when a third party, employed by neither the communicator nor the attorney, is present at the communication. The implication of the presence of such a third party is obvious; the client did not care whether the communication was kept confidential.

Regarding waiver of the privilege, the most common instance in which this occurs is when the communication itself becomes an important factor in the case. For example, if in a criminal case the defendant were to plead that she was acting as she did upon the advice of her attorney, then the content of the communications between the defendant and her attorney would certainly be relevant to establish whether she was acting in accordance with that advice and whether that advice was reasonable under the circumstances. This issue of introducing the communication into the case applies to almost all of the nonconstitutional privileges.

As with the case of the privilege against self-incrimination, it is currently disputed as to whether the attorney-client privilege applies to corporations. As noted above, it is my personal belief that this is inappropriate; nevertheless, the Supreme Court has so held.[2]

14.3 PHYSICIAN-PATIENT PRIVILEGE

The physician-patient privilege, like the attorney-client privilege, is based on the assumption that one gets the best advice if your advisor knows all of the facts. In this case the advice is being sought from a physician, not from a lawyer, but that does not change the public policy basis for the privilege. Notice that the Hippocratic oath is not part of the basis for this as a matter of law; that is a responsibility that doctors impose upon themselves.

Again, as with the attorney-client privilege, the physician-patient privilege can be waived. The most common instance of this, of course, is if the plaintiff files a suit for personal injuries sustained as a result of the defendant's action. When this is done, obviously, the plaintiff's medical history becomes relevant; if the injury preexisted the act of the defendant, then the plaintiff is not entitled to recover; similarly, if the plaintiff is "malingering" (legal terminology for faking it), then the plaintiff is not entitled to recover. Thus in personal injury cases the physician-patient privilege is held to be waived regarding all relevant medical records of the plaintiff. As with the attorney-client privilege, there appears to be a developing future crime exception to the physician-patient privilege, as well.[2]

14.4 OTHER PRIVILEGES

A whole series of other privileges exist. The most general of these are marital communications and governmental secrets, but many states have additional privileges that have been created by statute. The privilege for marital communications is based on the public policy grounds that spouses should feel free to communicate with each other and not be subject to forced testimony against each other. The privilege for governmental secrets comes in several subparts, which should be briefly mentioned.

The basic principle of this privilege is that there are certain things that the government, properly, can keep from having exposed to public view. The most common is that for military or diplomatic secrets, whose disclosure would be contrary to the public interest. The public policy basis of this, obviously, is the public interest. The problem that arises is, who determines whether disclosure would be against the public interest? In most cases, that decision is made by the judge before whom the evidence is sought to be introduced. There is also a privilege against the disclosure of grand jury proceedings, which means both the votes of the jurors and the testimony of witnesses. This privilege, however, is not nearly as absolute as any of the preceding ones, and judges may order disclosure when the circumstances so require. Other privileges include those relating to the files and investigations of law enforcement agencies and administrative agency deliberations. Both of these, however, have effectively been abrogated by statute at the federal level, by the Freedom of Information Act and the remainder of the Administrative Procedures Act, respectively.

Some jurisdictions have additional privileges, such as psychotherapist-patient, social worker-client, priest-penitent, etc. All of these cases are created by direct analogy to the physician-patient privilege and involve virtually identical limitations and provisions. The key point, however, is that these are not common law privileges and there must be a statute creating them in a particular jurisdiction before one of them can be asserted.[3]

REFERENCES

1.   Benjamin, M. & D. A. Bronstein, "Moral and Criminal Responsibility and Corporate Persons," in Samuels & Miller, eds., *Corporations and Society* (1987).
2.   *Tarasoff v. Bd. of Regents of Univ. of Cal.*, 55 P. 2d 334 (Ca. 1976).
3.   See, generally, Cleary, supra, ch. 12, n. 1; ch. 8—12.

15

Torts

Torts is the branch of the common law that deals with "civil wrongs." By this is meant injuries of a noncriminal nature to other parties. The term itself derives directly from the French; the French word for "wrong" is *tort*. In any tort action there are four fundamental things that must be proven by the plaintiff: duty, breach of duty, injury, and cause.

15.1 DUTY

The first thing that must be established in order for a plaintiff to win a tort suit is that the defendant owed the plaintiff a duty of some sort. Normally this duty is not spelled out explicitly in a statute, but is assumed as a duty that all owe to everyone else, i.e., the reasonable person. For example, we all have a duty to avoid injury to others when not threatened with injury ourselves, we all have a duty to obey traffic signals and signs, we all have a duty to operate our vehicles in a reasonable manner, etc. Nevertheless it is obligatory on the plaintiff in a tort suit to show that the defendant owed the plaintiff a duty of some sort.

15.2 BREACH OF DUTY

Having established that the plaintiff owed the defendant a duty, the plaintiff's next job is to show that the defendant failed to observe that duty, that he or she breached it. Normally this is done by showing that the defendant failed to take the necessary actions required to fulfill the duty, or took actions that violated the duty. In the most common type of tort case, the negligence case, all that is required is to show that the defendant was inattentive and negligently failed to observe the duty that he or she had.

15.3 INJURY

The third thing that the plaintiff must show is that the plaintiff was injured. If the plaintiff was not injured then there is no right to maintain an action. If the plaintiff cannot establish that there was an injury, then the plaintiff will be thrown out of court.

15.4 CAUSE

The last, and frequently the most contentious, issue in a tort suit is that of cause. The plaintiff must establish that the defendant's breach of duty caused the injuries sustained by the plaintiff. Cause in tort law has traditionally been of the "but-for" variety. By this was meant that the plaintiff had to show that but for the actions of the defendant, the plaintiff's injuries would not have occurred. In other words, but for the defendant's failing to stop at the stop sign, the plaintiff would not have been injured by the resulting collision of vehicles. Mere but-for causation, however, is not sufficient in modern law. Not only must there be but-for causation, but there must be "proximate" causation. The classic case that illustrates proximate causation, and this is not an imaginary case, runs something as follows:

- There is a man running down the railroad platform at the Long Island Railroad station in New York City. The Long Island Railroad station in New York City is a completely enclosed, underground railroad station. The person is running to try and catch a train that is slowly pulling out of the station. Seeing this potential passenger, the conductor leans out of one of the doors and offers his hand to help the person swing into the train. The person running down the platform grabs the conductor's hand and swings onto the train, but in the process of doing this drops a large paper bag that had been in his other arm.

  The paper bag, it turns out, was filled with fireworks. When it falls and hits the concrete platform, one of the fireworks goes off, which sets off all the other fireworks inside the bag, and now there are roman candles and sky rockets and pinwheels flying around in this total enclosed railroad station. It must have been quite a spectacular event. In any case, one of the fireworks, while flying around the station, hits one of the big old platform scales that hung from overhead hooks in railroad stations and knocks it off the hook. When the scale falls, it falls on Mrs. Palsgraf's foot and crushes it.

  Mrs. Palsgraf has been injured and wants to find somebody to recover from for her injuries. The person who was carrying the fireworks got on the train and has long since disappeared, and nobody knows who he was; Mrs. Palsgraf therefore decides to sue the Long Island Railroad.

Her allegations run along the following lines: If your conductor had not leaned out of the train to help this person onto the train, then the person would not have dropped the bag; if he had not dropped the bag, then the fireworks would not have gone off; if the fireworks had not gone off, then they would not have been flying around the station; if they were not flying around the station, then none of them could have hit the scale; if none of them could have hit the scale, then my foot would not have been injured. This was, it must be admitted, a perfectly legitimate train of "but-for" reasoning.

The case went all the way to the New York Court of Appeals, the highest court in New York, which ruled that Mrs. Palsgraf was not entitled to recover from the Long Island Railway on these facts. The court held that the breach of duty leading to the injury must be the proximate cause of the injury, not just the cause. Proximate cause, the court held, is determined by "reasonable foreseeability"; that is to say, the plaintiff must show that it is reasonably foreseeable that if the defendant commits this breach of duty, then the plaintiff would be injured in the way in which the plaintiff was injured. The court held, obviously, that the "Rube Goldberg-ish" chain of events outlined above was not reasonably foreseeable.[1]

As might be expected, the issue of proximate cause is one of the main areas of tension between lawyers and scientists at the moment. Lawyers need scientists of one type or another to come into court in many types of cases to establish that the proximate cause of the plaintiff's injury was the defendant's action. This becomes particularly difficult when we are dealing with major product liability cases such as bendectin, asbestos, diethylstilbestrol (DES), etc. It is also, obviously, a problem when we are dealing with suits filed by workers allegedly injured by a hazardous substance used in their place of employment or neighbors of hazardous waste sites (e.g., Love Canal, Woburn, etc.).

15.5 PERSONAL INJURY ACTIONS

The most common, at least in numbers, kind of tort suit is the personal injury suit. This is a suit in which the injury alleged is that to a particular person, normally to life, health, physical comfort, etc. The fact that it has its own name, *personal injury*, in no way distinguishes it from any other kind of tort suit.

15.6 NUISANCE AND TRESPASS

Two other kinds of tort suits are nuisance and trespass. Both involve damage to real property, but could also include personal injuries. They are frequently alleged in the same case, as the factual support for each of them could be very close.

Trespass involves interfering with another person's use of that other person's property by physically entering upon the land. Trespass, thus, requires that the defendant, or some agents or agency under the defendant's control, physically enter upon the plaintiff's land. Nuisance involves doing injury to plaintiff's property by action that does not occur on the plaintiff's property.

The classic and easily understood trespass case, of course, is the person who comes on your land and cuts down trees and carts them away and sells them. This is a person who has caused injury to your property by action taken on your property and is relatively easy to understand. A little more complicated is the problem of a neighborhood cement factory, which spews all sorts of particulate matter into the air, some of which lands on your property and causes damage to it. This too, however, has been held to be a trespass case. Somewhat more questionable, however, is the defendant who sprays not dust or particulate matter, but undetectable chemical residue on your property; the majority view, however, still is that this is a trespass.

Whether the last item would constitute a trespass or not, it would certainly constitute a nuisance. The defendant is taking activity on his property that results in diminution of the use and value of your property, a classic nuisance case. In the nuisance and trespass cases, the complaint is frequently filed seeking both money damages in tort and an injunction to prevent the defendant from repeating the actions that allegedly occurred. This is seeking alternative relief and, as discussed previously, is specifically provided for in the rules of procedure.

15.7 OTHER TORTS

There are innumerable other torts that could be mentioned at this point: defamation, false imprisonment, malicious prosecution, malicious interference with business relationship, etc., but we have neither the time nor the space to discuss any of these in any detail. We do, however, need to briefly mention products liability, "absolute liability," and "malpractice."

15.7.1 Products Liability

A products liability case is a case in which it is alleged that the defendant manufactured or produced a product that was defective and, when it failed, caused injury to the plaintiff. In this sense, obviously, it is a straightforward tort case. The thing that makes a products liability case somewhat different is that there need be no direct connection between the plaintiff injured person and the original manufacturer or producer of the allegedly defective object. In the normal course of business, that allegedly defective object will have passed through many hands before it gets anywhere near the plaintiff. It will have been manufactured, sold to a wholesaler, sold to a retailer, and then bought by the plaintiff or, maybe, bought by the plaintiff's employer and then given to the plaintiff to use. It is this long chain of intervening parties that makes the products liability case different from the normal tort case.

15.7.2 Absolute Liability

Absolute liability is truly different from the normal tort case; in a case alleging absolute liability, the duty and breach of duty requirements of a normal tort case are dispensed with and the plaintiff merely has to prove injury and that the injury was caused by the defendant's actions.

The classic absolute liability case (classic because it is the first one) was decided in England in the 1860s. It involved the construction of a dam that failed and caused a flood downstream. The court in that case held that building a dam and impounding waters was an inherently dangerous activity, which could reasonably be anticipated to result in injury to downstream parties and, since the benefit of the structure was derived solely by the constructing party, the constructing party would be absolutely liable for injuries that occurred to others.[2]

Another example of an absolute liability case involved the farmer who hired a crop-spraying helicopter being held liable to his neighbors when the crop spray drifted across (or, perhaps, was incorrectly sprayed) onto the neighbor's property. The court looked at the idea of pesticide spraying, held that this was an inherently dangerous activity, and therefore held that the requirements to impose absolute liability on the defendant were met.[3]

15.8 Malpractice

There is only one difference between a malpractice suit and an ordinaty lawsuit — the extent of the duty owed by the defendant to the plaintiff. In a malpractice case the defendant is, if not an expert at least holding itself out to be one, and so the duty of case is greater than that imposed on a normal "reasonable" defendant.

The biggest problem that a plaintiff faces in a malpractice suit is establishing what the standard of care is, i.e., what duty was owed by the defendant to the plaintiff. Traditionally the courts used what was called the "locality" standard — the defendant had to exercise that degree of care that would be expected from similar professionals in that locality. In the past 40 years, however, the courts have been moving toward a "professional" or "national" standard — the degree of care that would be exercised by those holding themselves out to be experts of the same type, without regard to the geographical location.

In establishing the standard of care, then, as in establishing proximate cause in complicated scientific cases, the courts need to hear from expert witnesses. This is one of the most frequent uses of expert witnesses, and both of the parties and the courts are truly dependent on their being available and being able to testify effectively.[4]

The law of torts is, like all of the common law, constantly changing. The development of refinements in the area of products liability, absolute liability, etc. is preceding apace. These are nonstatutory changes in the law, and for that reason it is relatively difficult for nonlawyers to keep up with them, as newspapers do not do a particularly good job of covering court decisions. Nevertheless, it is hoped that you now have some background in the area of the law of torts.

REFERENCES

1. *Palsgraf v. Long Island R. Co.*, 162 N.E. 99 (N.Y. 1926).
2. *Rylands v. Fletcher*, L.R. 3 H.L. 330 (1868).
3. *Langan v. Valicopters*, 567 P. 2d 218 (Wash. 1977).
4. For a discussion of how to be such a witness, see Matson, J. V., *Effective Expert Witnessing: A Handbook for Technical Professionals* (1990), CRC Press, Boca Raton, FL.

16

Contracts

As a matter of law, a contract is nothing more than an agreement of two or more parties to engage in certain future acts. The agreement must be given freely, willingly, and without coercion. The agreement need not be reduced to writing, except under the special instances mentioned later in the discussion of the "statute of frauds."

16.1 MEETING OF THE MINDS

A contract is created when it can be determined that there has been a meeting of the minds, i.e., it can be determined that the parties to the contract have reached agreement as to the substance thereof. Normally a contract negotiation is, in law, broken down into two parts: the offer and the acceptance.

An offer is just that, — the statement that the party making it is willing to enter into a contract on certain specified terms. The offer may be made to one individual or to the public at large; it does not matter which. If I publish an advertisement in the newspaper that says any individual who phones a given phone number between the hours of 1 and 2 p.m. next Monday will receive $30, that is an offer; anyone who phones that telephone number has then accepted the offer and is entitled to the money. If I should refuse to pay, I would be in breach of contract and could successfully be sued in court.

As indicated above, an acceptance can be indicated either by verbal agreement or by action indicating acceptance of the offer. The telephone example above is an act indicating acceptance of the offer. A verbal acceptance is simply to say to somebody, "I accept your offer" and that is then a contract. In the real world, of course, we very rarely accept the first proposal made when negotiating a contract. If A says to B "here are my terms," and B says "well that is all fine and good except for ..." and quibbles about one or two of the items, B is considered to have made a new (counter-) offer to A. A now has the right to either accept or make another offer. Assuming that there is an eventual "meeting of the minds," this can go on indefinitely until we have a contract.

16.2 STATUTE OF FRAUDS

It should be obvious at this point that a contract does not have to be written. Verbal contracts, or contracts evidenced by actions, are just as enforceable as written contracts as a general rule. The exceptions to the general rule are those listed in the *statute of frauds*, a statute passed in England many centuries ago, which has been incorporated into the common law in the United States.

The main point of the statute of frauds is that certain types of contracts must be in writing; failure to reduce them to writing makes them totally unenforceable. The most important of these contracts are contracts affecting an interest in land and contracts for personal services that do not anticipate completion within one year. These and many other types of contracts must be reduced to writing in order to become enforceable.

16.3 "MERGER" CLAUSES

If a contract is going to be reduced to writing, it frequently contains a *merger clause*. This is a clause that states something along the lines of "this written agreement constitutes the full agreement between the parties and nothing that is not included herein is incorporated into this agreement." The point of this clause is to prevent one party or the other from saying "that's not all we agreed to, we also agreed to x, y, and z." A merger clause states that there are no things left out of the written agreement that are involved in the matter.

16.4 CONTRACTS OF ADHESION

In the real world, of course, we do not necessarily bargain before we enter into any sort of agreement. In most cases, in fact, we have a "take it or leave it" situation; either we can buy the item or contract for the services at the price the seller or provider wants to charge or we can not buy or not contract. We do not have the ability to bargain over the terms of the agreement. A contract of this sort, in which the bargaining power of the two parties is quite disparate, is called a *contract of adhesion*. By this it is meant that a person gets a chance to adhere to it or not to adhere to it, but does not get the chance to bargain about it. Contracts of adhesion are construed strictly against the interest of the party who drafts them, and, if they are found to be "unconscionable," the entire agreement can be set aside by a court.

16.5 WARRANTIES

A warranty is an assurance given by one party to another that certain things are true or will happen, etc. In contract actions the most common warranties are of "merchantability" and "fitness for a particular purpose." The warranty of merchantability, which is implied to exist in all contracts unless it is specifically excluded, states that the item being transferred or services being provided will be of the average quality of such items as normally dealt in. The presumption of merchantability can be defeated by words such as "as is" or "without any warranties, expressed or implied."

The warranty of fitness for a particular purpose is a more difficult warranty. Let us assume that I were to walk into a paint store and talk to a person there to find out what would be the best type of paint to use in painting the exterior of my house in Michigan. That person then sells me a very high priced, very fancily tinted interior latex paint. I use this paint on my house and, one year later, find it all washing and peeling off; it was interior paint, not exterior paint. I would then try to sue the paint store on the grounds of breaching the warranty of fitness for a particular purpose. I am not claiming that the paint was inferior, merely that I relied on their expertise and I told them the purpose for which I intended to use the paint and they sold me paint that was not fit for the purpose. Assuming that I could prove all of this, I could win a suit based on the warranty of fitness for a particular purpose.

16.6 BREACH OF CONTRACT

As noted above, a suit that is filed when somebody fails to live up to a contract is called a *suit for breach of contract*. It is a civil suit, and a suit of its own classification; it is not a subdivision of a tort suit, for example. In a breach of contract action, one need prove only the terms of the contract, that the terms were not adhered to, that the plaintiff suffered injury, and that the injury was caused by the breach of the terms of the contract. All reasonably foreseeable injuries are compensable under a breach of contract suit unless there is what is called a *liquidated damages clause* in the original contract.

A liquidated damages clause is a clause in a contract that says "if this contract is breached by party A, party A will pay to party B X dollars; if this contract is breached by party B, party B will pay party A Y dollars." It is liquidated damages because it provides for the amount of money that will be paid in advance and thus liquidates (converts into cash) a subsequent judgment.

16.7 SPECIFIC PERFORMANCE

In a contract action, one can not only seek monetary damages, but one can also seek specific performance of the contract. This is, in effect, an injunction forcing the other party to live up to the terms of the contract. Specific performance is available only if the items involved in the contract are unique.

By this it is meant, for example, that if I contract with somebody else to buy 20 reams of paper of a given grade and they refuse to give them to me when I tender payment, I will not be able to get specific performance, as it is perfectly possible to measure my damages by the cost of buying the same paper from another supplier. On the other hand, if I contract to buy a particular race horse and the other party fails to deliver the horse to me when I present the money, there is no other equivalent race horse in existence. (This is true, no matter how bad the race horse may be, as I contracted for a particular horse.) In the latter case, I would be entitled to specific performance.

As can be seen from the above discussion, the law of contracts is not simple. In fact, it is one of the few full-year courses that law students take in their first year of law school. The above discussion, obviously, only introduces a few of the pertinent terms. A summary piece of advice is, if you are involved in an important contract, negotiate the terms with the other side, but then have a lawyer examine it to make sure it really says what you think you have negotiated.

17

Insurance

For this general discussion of insurance law, the world of insurance can be divided into five basic types: property and casualty, life and health, maritime, bonding and surety, and workers compensation. Each of these divisions, of course, can be subdivided into many, many parts. Property and casualty, for example, can be divided up at the first level into title, fire, homeowners, automobile, general liability, etc. There are, however, a few principles of insurance law that are common to all of these.

17.1 INTERPRETATION OF INSURANCE CONTRACTS

An insurance agreement between an insurance company and its insured is a contract. As such, it is interpreted along the lines of most contracts. An insurance contract of the type that any reader of this book would normally purchase is, obviously, a contract of adhesion. As such it follows the general rule of such contracts; it is interpreted strictly against the party that drew it up (the insurance company) if there is a conflict regarding the meaning of the terms. At the present time (1990), for example, there is a great deal of legal controversy regarding whether environmental problems are covered under a company's normal general comprehensive liability policy. Since the language used in such policies was drafted long before environmental cleanup became a major problem, the policies are generally either void of language on the subject or use unclear language. The result has been a tendency on the part of the courts to find coverage for the insured in such cases.

Like any contract, the insurance contract can be voided by the insurance company if false information is given on the application for insurance. This is an example of fraud in the contract, and it is the insurance company's duty, as a general rule, to prove that the information was false and that this false information lead them to issue the insurance policy, by "clear and convincing" evidence. In this respect, insurance policies are interpreted in the same way as contracts, except for the requirement that the false information furnished has had a "material" effect on the decision to issue the policy.

17.2 INSURANCE COMPANIES

In the United States there are basically two kinds of insurance companies, profit-making and mutual. A profit-making insurance company is simply that — an organization that is in the business of selling insurance policies while at the same time making profits for its owners. Many of the large U.S. insurance companies (e.g., Aetna, Hartford) are of this kind. In this type of insurance company the risk money is put up by the stockholders in the hopes of achieving profits based on the experience of the company. This is most common in the fields of property and casualty, bonding and surety, and maritime insurance.

Mutual insurance companies are companies that have management elected by the policy holders, and any profits realized are returned to the policy holders. This is not to say these are small companies (e.g., Mutual of Omaha), it is merely to indicate that they are a different type of company. In a mutual company the money is contributed by the policy holders in the form of their premiums, and they have voting rights to employ the directors, officers, etc. Mutual companies are most commonly found in the life and health insurance fields, although they can and do participate in the other fields.

17.3 REINSURANCE AND SELF-INSURANCE

Other aspects of insurance law that should be briefly mentioned are reinsurance and self-insurance. In reinsurance one insurance company "sells" all or part of the risk it is assuming to another insurance company. The agreement under which this sale occurs is, for reasons I do not know, called a *treaty*, Reinsurance is very common on large risks, e.g., where the original insurance company does not want to assume the entire possible risk of having to pay a claim and seeks to spread this risk with other insurance companies. This most frequently occurs in the fields of property and casualty, and maritime insurance, but can occur in any of the fields.

Self-insurance is very simple. A company that has a great deal of cash reserves does not need to take out insurance if it is willing to assume the risk of loss on its own. Self-insurance can occur in any of the fields of insurance if the company engaging in the operation is willing to assume the risk.

17.4 MARITIME INSURANCE

As the name implies, maritime insurance is devoted to the question of shipping goods by sea. It is, without a doubt, the oldest kind of insurance known; there is a belief that some tablets found in Ur and Dilmun reflect maritime insurance agreements in the 24th or 25th century B.C. A ship owner will take what is called *hull insurance* insuring the vessel itself against loss. The ship owner may also take *carriage* insurance, insuring the goods that the ship is carrying so that, if the ship were lost and the owners of the goods were to sue the ship owner for their loss, the ship owner would be protected. The owner of the goods, too, can take insurance against the possible loss of the goods in transit. Maritime insurance is generally written on an individual basis. By this we mean that each insurance contract is separately designed to suit the circumstances of the particular ship, the particular goods, the particular voyage to be engaged in, etc. In this respect, then, maritime insurance is somewhat different from the standard insurance contract of adhesion, as individual policies are frequently tailored to particular ships and voyages.

17.5 BONDING AND SURETY

A surety is a person or organization that is willing to put its money behind another person or organization's performance of a given act. The most common instance of surety insurance is that of contractors and subcontractors on construction projects. As a rule the general contractor will require surety bonds from each of the subcontractors, and the owner of the building will require a surety bond from the general contractor. The purpose of the surety bond is to provide for the completion of the required work, even if the party who is suppose to perform it fails to perform it. In the event of nonperformance of the contract, the surety has the right to either finish the work itself (usually by hiring another contractor) or pay the money guaranteed by the insurance contract to the person in whose favor the contract runs so that person can hire another contractor to have the work finished.

Bonding is similar to suretyship, except it more generally applies to individuals performing certain acts. Remember from our discussion many chapters ago regarding equity issues in court that the court can require that the person seeking a temporary restraining order or a preliminary injunction post a bond to compensate the other party in case that proves necessary. This would normally be done by securing a bond from an insurance company. The insurance agreement would say that if certain events come to pass, then the insurance company will pay the money to the party in whose favor the bond runs. The most common use of bonds, however, is to insure against wrongful acts of employees in sensitive positions, e.g., bank officers, corporate officers, and, of course, insurance company officers. In these cases, if the employee misappropriates money, the insurance company will compensate the employer for the loss.

In both bonds and sureties, the insurance company retains the right to recover its money from the person who secured the policy. In other words, if a subcontractor fails to perform the contract as specified, the surety company has the right, after paying the amount of the policy to the person in whose favor the insurance runs, to sue the subcontractor to get back the money it had to pay. The same thing is true of a bond: the bonding company can proceed against the individual who violates its terms. In other words, all that a surety or a bonding insurance contract provides is that the insurer will, so to speak, temporarily lend the money to the insured to pay off what is required, and then will get the money back from the insured after it has been paid.

17.6 LIFE AND HEALTH

I doubt that very much time needs to be spent on this subject, as I suspect that all members of the intended audience for this book have encountered life and/or health insurance. Life insurance, of course, comes in several varieties: whole, term, etc. I will not try to explain the details of these here, but merely suggest that you consult your own insurance agent.

Health insurance, of course, is another type of entity. In health insurance, the insurer agrees to pay those medical costs that might be incurred that are covered by the policy. In disability insurance, the insurer agrees to pay a certain sum to, normally, make up for income the insured will lose due to an injury.

The thing that makes life and health insurance a separate field is that the underwriting (the decision whether to grant or deny a policy) is much more exact in this area than in almost any other area of the insurance industry. There are very fine, enormously detailed statistics regarding the life expectancy of individuals in all sorts of situations, and the types of diseases, injuries, etc. to which they might be prone. For this reason the two types of insurance are grouped together in normal discussion, as there are a huge amount of actuarial data available to make the insurance decision.

17.7 WORKER'S COMPENSATION

One of the traditional common law rules was the *fellow servant* doctrine, under which an employee could not sue his employer for injuries sustained as the result of the actions of another employee. As a consequence of this doctrine, all of the states and the federal government have adopted statutes called, in one form or another, workman's compensation, which provide for the medical expenses of injured employees and, if the injury is permanent, for compensation to them. Since the potential amount of damages that might be awarded for a permanent injury under workman's compensation statutes is normally fixed in the legislation, e.g., the loss of a finger is a worth $X, the loss of a hand $Y, the loss of an arm $Z, it is relatively easy for insurance companies to figure their potential exposure and thus set the rates for that portion of the employer's compensation insurance. The medical expenses part, obviously, is rated in the same way that health insurance is rated. Again, as with any other type of insurance, the employer can self-insure; in this case, self-insurance is allowed only if the employer can convince the state agency in charge of the statute that it has sufficient funds to do so.

17.8 PROPERTY AND CASUALTY INSURANCE

This last field of insurance to be discussed, of course, is one that we are all concerned about, just as we are about life and health insurance. It is, however, a somewhat more complicated area of insurance law, and we shall discuss several of the issues involved.

As a general rule, most of us purchase combined property and casualty insurance. A typical homeowners policy, for example, is property insurance in that it protects against loss in the event of fire, robbery, etc., and is also casualty insurance as it says that the insurance company will defend on our behalf any suit filed against us arising out of our use of the property (e.g., a delivery person falling on our icy front steps) and will pay any award granted up to the limits of that section of the policy. Automobile policies are the same: one carries collision and comprehensive coverage to protect the vehicle and liability coverage in the event that third parties are injured through our operation of the vehicle.

17.8.1 Primary and Excess Insurance

In many cases an insured, especially major insureds such as manufacturing corporations, can get a better rate on the cost of their insurance by dividing the policy into two parts, referred to as primary and excess insurance. The primary insurance is written up to a certain limit, i.e., the insurance company will provide defense and pay any award up to the policy limit. The excess insurance will cover any award in excess of the amount of that covered by the primary insurance up to yet another limit. By dividing the potential loss in this way, it is sometimes possible to get a better rate for the total insurance package than one could if one placed the entire risk in one policy.

Self-insurance is also a form of dividing the risk into primary and excess. If one carries a $250 deductible on one's automobile collision policy, then the vehicle owner is the primary insurer (up to the limit of $250) and the automobile insurance company is the excess carrier (all damages above $250). A deductible on an insurance policy, then, is legally equivalent to having the insured carry the primary coverage for that loss as a self-insurer. Of course a major corporation would do it very differently; something along the lines of "we will assume all loss up to 250 thousand, 500 thousand," etc., and the insurance company will assume the risk above that amount.

The insured is also a self-insurer for all damages or problems that exceed the limits of the insurance policies, whether it be only primary, or primary and excess. If there is a potential for an award in excess of the policy limits, it is an excellent idea for the insured to retain its own lawyer so that it does not lose in the transaction the money that it might be required to be paid in excess of the policy limits.

The payment of money when and if an event specified in the insurance agreement occurs is what is referred to as the *duty to pay*; the other part of a liability insurance agreement is the *duty to defend*, which we shall now consider.

17.8.2 Duty to Defend

One of the things that one contracts for when securing a liability insurance policy is for the insurance company to assume the costs of defending the insured against any legal action that may arise. Thus, if you are involved in automobile accident and are sued, the insurance will provide a lawyer on your behalf. It may not, however, be the lawyer you would choose if you were free to choose your own lawyer, as most insurance policies issued to individuals say that the insurance company has the full control over the course of litigation.

A major issue in contemporary environmental insurance situations is, what triggers the duty to defend? There have been quite a few cases in the past 10 years concerning whether the duty to defend arises when a government agency files a notice of violation of an environmental standard or whether it does not arise until some later point in the process, e.g., when an administrative proceeding is instituted, when an administrative order is entered directing certain actions, or only when the issue eventually reaches a court. The courts in the many states seem to be going in very different directions on this issue.

17.8.3 Good Faith and Fair Dealing

Since under the duty to defend the insurance company has control over the litigation, the courts have imposed upon insurance companies a duty to do so in good faith and to deal fairly with the insured. The issue of the duty of good faith and fair dealing can arise in two types of situations, referred to as first party and third party. The first party refers to a fight between the insured and the insurance company for failure to pay a claim, normally a property damage claim. If your home owners insurance company refuses to pay a claim you make for a burglary on the grounds that they do not believe that a burglary occurred, or refuses to pay a claim for a fire loss on the ground that it was arson, then we have a first-party dispute. It is called a *first party* because the fight is between the insured (the first party) and the insurance company (the second party). A third-party claim arises when the insurance company does not do an adequate or fair job of defending you against a claim made by some other person (the third party).

The most common first-party dispute, of course, is that of failure to pay when it is required by the contract. This is not limited, obviously, to the property and casualty field; first party claims can occur in any field of insurance. If a suit is filed against an insurance company on a first-party claim, the relief normally sought is not just payment of the claim but also any additional injury that the insured may have incurred and, perhaps, punitive damages.

Other costs the insured might have incurred, for example, would include such things as the necessity to sell the car in order to pay a medical bill that the insurance company refused to pay, in which case the insured would seek the value of the car that was lost. If the insured, for example, had to borrow money in order to rebuild a house on which the insurance company refuses to pay the fire insurance claim, then interest and points paid would be part of the claim as such consequential damages. The possibility of punitive damages arises if it can be shown that the insurance company was either grossly negligent in its refusal to pay the claim or did so in bad faith. Both of these terms, *gross negligence* and *bad faith*, are legal terms of art, and books could be written in the attempt to define them, so we will not attempt to do so here.

Third-party claims, obviously only arise in the liability situation. The most common of these is when an insurance company refuses to settle a liability claim for an amount within the policy limit and a judgment is subsequently entered against the insured for more than the policy limit. If the insured can show that the insurer was given the opportunity to settle the case within the policy limits, and either recklessly or willfully and maliciously failed to do so, then the insured can recover the full amount of the adverse judgment, even the part that is in excess of the policy limit. In fact, it is not at all infrequent for a party against whom such an excess judgment is entered to assign his or her right to file a third-party claim against the insurance company to the third party who won the original judgment in return for being released from that judgment, or from having that judgment at least suspended until the outcome of the suit against the insurer. In either case, however, there has been a judgment entered against the insured and it can very severely affect such things as credit ratings, ability to continue operations, etc. For this reason, again, if there is a real potential for excess liability ending up upon the insured, the insured should retain its own counsel to participate in any proceedings.

18

Real Property

Real property is basic in its importance, and there are obviously special rules in real property law. The single most important of these has been discussed previously, the requirement of the statute of frauds that any contract affecting an interest in real property be in writing. It is for this reason that sales of property or leases of property are almost always in writing. In addition, all states have what are called *title record systems*, which require that major actions affecting the title and use of real property be recorded, normally at the county level, with a public agency, where they are open to inspection by all. We will first look at deeds, which are the documents that are recorded in title record systems.

18.1 WARRANTY DEEDS

As the previous chapter indicated, a *warranty* is merely the legal term for what in general usage is referred to as a guarantee. A person who signs and grants a warranty deed to a second person is, in effect, stating, "I guarantee that I owe the below described interest in the property, and that I am transferring it to you subject to only those restrictions that are specifically stated in this deed." Any restrictions upon the property or, as they are called, *clouds upon title*, must be specified in a warranty deed. If they were not specified, then the person who granted the warranty deed would be liable to the recipient of the deed for failing to live up to the warranties contained in the instrument.

The warranty deed, then, is the strongest assurance one can receive that one is receiving exactly what one bargains for when securing an interest in real property.

18.2 QUITCLAIM DEED

The other major form of deed to real property is called a quitclaim deed. In a quitclaim deed the grantor merely states something along the lines of "I hereby give to you all of my title to this property, whatever that title may be." The standard terminology that appears in a quitclaim deed says something along the lines of "X hereby grants unto Y all of his right title and interest in the property known as Black Acre." Notice that nothing is said about what that right, title, and interest might be, merely that, whatever it be, it is now given to the other party. A quitclaim deed, then, is obviously considerably weaker protection to the grantee than is a warranty deed.

18.3 THE EXTENT OF OWNERSHIP OF REAL PROPERTY

The traditional common law view is that the owner of a piece of property owns everything below that property to the center of the earth and everything above it to the end of the universe. Obviously, however, this requires some qualification, as it would be very difficult, considering the rotation of the earth on its axis and the rotation of the planet around the sun, not to mention the rotation of the galaxy, etc., to locate the position of the property in relation to the universe.

In actual fact, in U.S. law, one has the right to occupy the air space above one's property (subject to any zoning or other governmental limitations that might be applied), but one does not have the right to exclude other persons above an altitude of 500 feet from the ground unless one is actually occupying that area. This is the *public right of air passage* and was defined by the Supreme Court in a famous case.[1]

The traditional analogy of property rights is to a bundle of sticks, each stick representing one aspect of the rights that one has in real property when one owns it. The most primitive of these sticks is that of bare ownership. The next most important is that of the right to occupy the surface of the land, and the next most important is the right to extract things from beneath the surface of the land, etc.[2] Each of these rights can be granted away to another party; for example, if one sells the mineral rights in general, or the right to explore for and exploit oil deposits, or the right to extract iron ore, one is granting away part of one's rights to exploit the subsurface. If one grants a long-term lease of the surface of the property, one is giving away one's right to occupy and to use the surface of the property, etc. As is obvious from these examples, one can give away all of the "bundle of sticks" by granting the entire property to someone else, one can give away any one of the bundle of sticks, or one can give away a portion of one of the bundle of sticks.

Any grant of any of these rights, being something that affects the title to the property, is required by most states to be by deed and to be recorded in the land records office. Any such grant becomes what was referred to above as a cloud upon the title; in other words, it means that any grantee will not receive the full bundle of sticks, but only a partial bundle.

One of the most common pieces of the bundle that is granted away is the right to use and occupy a small segment of the surface. This is what is generally called an easement. An easement is the right of another party to use the surface for some purpose of its own, to the exclusion of the owner of the underlying property. Normally an easement is given for roads, driveways, electric power lines, pipelines, etc., but an easement can be granted for any reason, or for none. All that is required is that the easement be recorded in the land records office.

A typical easement, and this is a real example (the author's own house) might have something along these lines. There is an easement 100 feet wide across the property under which (10 feet under the ground) is buried a gasoline transmission pipeline belonging to an oil company. The owner of the easement, the oil company, has the right to come in and do repairs, replacement, etc. to the pipeline, after giving the owner of the overlying property (me) 30 days notice of its intent to do this. The oil company is under an obligation to replace any tree, shrub, etc. that it might destroy in the process of doing its work, but the owner of the property does not have the right to build any sort of structures (or anything else) upon the surface of the easement. The easement in this particular case had been granted by a predecessor owner of the property on which our house is built; in fact, it was granted three owners before we bought the property, before anyone had thought of building a house on the property, at a time when it was still farmland.

All such limitations that we have discussed so far upon the rights of the owner of real property are those that are recorded and in some way granted. There is another way in which the rights of the owner of a piece of real property can be diminished, and that is by adverse possession.

18.4 ADVERSE POSSESSION

Adverse possession is the loss by the owner of the property to another party of a part of the bundle of property rights that the owner originally had. It occurs when another party, "openly, actually, notoriously, exclusively, and continuously" occupies the property, without the permission of the owner, under the claim that the party in occupation has the right to do so and the owner does not have the right to exclude him.[3] Furthermore, this occupation must continue uninterruptedly for a period designated by the legislature and commonly referred to as the *statute of repose*. In most states this period is something between 12 and 20 years, and any individual state can make it longer or shorter at the choice of the legislature.

18.5 GOVERNMENTAL LIMITATIONS ON PROPERTY RIGHTS

There are many ways in which one's right to real property can be and are restricted by governmental agencies. The right of the public to air navigation, mentioned above, is one. Here we shall consider some others.

18.5.1 Eminent Domain

The government, by its mere existence as a government, always has the right to condemn (take) private property for public use. This is called the *right of eminent domain*, and the action by which it is effected is called *condemnation*.

The Fifth Amendment to the Constitution says "nor shall private property be taken for public use without just compensation." A question that frequently arose in the past was whether the government had the right to give its power of eminent domain to nongovernmental entities, such as railroads, electric companies, etc. The courts have held yes, indeed, a properly adopted and drafted legislative act can give the right of eminent domain to private entities, provided that the private entity is going to act for the general public good.

18.5.2 Zoning and Planning

Zoning ordinances and planning requirements, obviously, also impose restrictions upon one's use of land. This is not the place to discuss these issues in any detail, as there have been enormous treatises written on the subject. Nevertheless, a few brief topics should be mentioned.

The ordinance pursuant to which the governmental limitation is imposed must be enacted under the *police powers*. The police powers are those powers that belong to state and local governments for the purpose of "protecting the public health, safety, welfare and morals." In a landmark case in the 1920s, the U.S. Supreme Court held that zoning and planning ordinances would meet the test of being within the police powers.[4]

If the limitations imposed are such as to deprive the owner of all reasonable use of the land, then the courts may hold that the government has, in effect, condemned the land and must pay compensation as required by the Fifth Amendment to the owner. These cases normally are begun by the landowner filing a suit for what is called *inverse condemnation*. It is called *inverse* because the government is not filing the action to condemn the land, the landowner is filing the action claiming that the government had condemned the land but has not paid compensation.

There are many other things about real property that could be discussed, but they would require a full book to do so. For those interested in this matter, whether just out of curiosity or because, like the author, they are land owners themselves, there are numerous texts available.

REFERENCES

1. *U.S. v. Causby*, 328 U.S. 256 (1946).
2. Barlowe, R., *Land Resource Economics*, 4th ed. (1986), ch. 12.
3. See, e.g., *Davids v. Davis*, 445 N.W. 2d 460 (Mich. App. 1989).
4. *Village of Euclid v. Ambler Realty Co.*, 272 U.S. 365 (1926).

19

Environmental Law

Since environmental law is what the author of this book teaches, this chapter could, if he let himself go, go on forever. However, as the publisher of this book is in the process of issuing a series of volumes devoted to specific issues in environmental law, I will restrain myself. Instead of giving a detailed discussion of various environmental statutes, issues, etc., I will give vent to some thoughts of my own, as well as giving a sort of taxonomic classification of the issues that occur in environmental law.

19.1 WHAT IS ENVIRONMENTAL LAW?

One of the problems in dealing with *environmental law* is attempting to define exactly what is meant by the term. In the very early days it was clear what was meant — protection of the environment per se. By this I mean that the early laws, such as the original Clean Air Act, the Federal Water Pollution Control Act, the National Environmental Policy Act, and the Endangered Species Act, were designed to protect the physical and biological environment for its own sake, not as something used by people. Thus, under the original Clean Air Act, it was believed that the "secondary ambient air quality standards" would be stricter than the "primary" standards, as the secondary standards were devoted to protecting welfare, whereas the primary ones were devoted to health. In those days (the late 1960s and early 1970s) it was felt that humans were polluting the environment and were destroying it, even if we were not endangering ourselves.

It is clear that, since the mid-1970s, the focus of what is called environmental law has changed considerably. The emphasis is now upon danger to people and not on the preservation of the environment for the sake of the birds, the bees, and the fish. Thus such statues as the Safe Drinking Water Act, the Resource Conservation and Recovery Act, and the Comprehensive Environmental Response, Compensation, and Liability Act ("superfund") are clearly directed at issues of human health rather than environmental preservation. It is my personal belief that this change has occurred because environmentalists, in their political efforts to protect the birds, the bees, and the fish, found it expedient to emphasize potential dangers to people in order to secure passage of the statutes.

This, then, leaves us with several questions. Where, for example, does one classify the Occupational Safety and Health Act (OSHA)? Is it an environmental statute, or not? How about the Food, Drug and Cosmetic Act (FDCA)? The Mine Safety Act? The Consumer Product Safety Act? The list, obviously, could go on for some time. In my personal classification, for example, OSHA and the Consumer Product Safety Act do not qualify as environmental statutes, whereas some small parts of the Food, Drug and Cosmetic Act and the Mine Safety Act do. On the other hand, when I teach a class (every other year) in toxic substance law, time is spent on the FDCA, OSHA, and Consumer Product Safety Act. Therefore, please remember that you are receiving, in what follows, a discussion and distinctions from a person who is not sure exactly what should or should not be included in this chapter.

One of the fundamental distinctions that can be drawn in environmental law is between what I would refer to as *management statutes* and *regulatory statutes*. The management statutes deal with how things are to be done by the government when it is a primary government activity that is affecting the environment. The regulatory statutes deal with how the government regulates the activities of other parties that affect the environment. What follows, then, is going to be, basically, a listing of agencies and statutes with, where I feel it appropriate, a few brief comments regarding them. This will be confined to the federal government, since, for obvious reasons, I cannot go through all 50 states and discuss them, not to mention the many multistate interstate compacts that also exist.

19.2 MANAGEMENT DUTIES

Department of Agriculture

- U.S. Forest Service
    The Forest Service, of course, is responsible for managing all of the lands in the national forest system. Under amendments to the "Organic Act" of the Forest Service in the 1970s, the Forest Service is responsible for managing these lands for not only sustained yield of timber and timber products, but also for environmental

amenities and values such as scenery, soil protection, and wilderness.

- Soil Conservation Service

     The Soil Conservation Service is responsible for aiding farms and local governments to prevent soil erosion by both air (wind) and water. In the latter duties, particularly, the Soil Conservation Service is actively involved in building small dams, terraces, and other similar types of retaining structures and can have significant impacts on a local area's environment.

Department of Defense

The Department of Defense, of course, is a very major land owning unit of the federal government; all forts, bases and military reservations fall under the management of one of the divisions of the Department of Defense. Although the Department of Defense is expected to comply with environmental statutes as a general rule, it is sometimes exempted, either in toto or by presidential proclamation stating that particular environmental regulations will not be applied to a particular area for national security reasons. One of the major problems of monitoring what the Department of Defense does on its lands is that many of them are closed to the public for safety reasons or the activities undertaken there are not publicized for national security reasons.

- Corps of Engineers

     The Army Corps of Engineers are the sole federal "beavers" in the eastern U.S. and share this role with WAPA in the west. The Corps is also responsible for maintaining the navigability of rivers and harbors, and thus does a great deal of dredging.

Department of Energy

The Department of Energy has many functions that directly affect the environment. It is responsible for research on alternate energy technologies, some of which, if they were to prove out, might prove environmentally less damaging than current technologies. It is responsible for managing the emergency petroleum reservoirs that are supposedly being filled with imported oil against the prospect of future embargoes. It is also responsible for other activities as a land owner, including its currently environmentally most difficult one, that of providing materials for nuclear weapons while at the same time running the plants that produce these materials in an environmentally safe manner.

Department of Health and Human Services

While neither a major management agency nor a regulator, the normal, day-to-day activities of many units of this department directly affect various environmental activities. The Centers for Disease Control in the Public Health Service, of course, is the primary epidemiological investigatory agency of the federal government. As such it investigates complaints of "environmentally induced" illnesses. It also has a subdivision, the Agency for Toxic Substances and Disease Control, created by the Superfund Amendments and Reauthorization Act, which is designed to track what happens near superfund sites. In addition, the National Institutes of Health, also part of the Department, clearly play major roles in evaluating issues of causation of various illnesses from environmental exposures.

Department of the Interior

- Bureau of Land Management (BLM)
    The BLM is responsible to manage a very expansive territory in the West, primary grazing land, but some of it forested. In the same way that the Forest Service's mandate was amended slightly in the 1970s so was that of the Bureau of Land Management. One of the principal problems that faces the bureau is that its land is leased out under "grazing permits" for private use, so BLM is both an owner-manager and a regulator of private activities.
- Fish and Wildlife Service (FWS)
    The FWS is the part of Department of the Interior that manages the national wildlife refuges and game areas. As such it is a management agency whose primary purpose is to promote healthy wildlife. At times, however, it has come into conflict in this aim with the desire to, for example, explore for oil on its lands.
- National Park Service
    The Park Service, of course, administers the national parks and monuments. The management conflicts it always faces are between encouraging tourism development and amenities, and preserving intact ecosystems as part of the parks. The Yellowstone Park fires of recent vintage are a clear indicator of the types of problems that can arise when faced with these conflicting aims.
- Water and Power Administration
    This is the successor agency to the former Bureau of Reclamation. As such it is one of the major constructors, operators, and owners of large dams in the western United States. In addition to the environmental problems that can arise in deciding to build a dam, it faces problems in the management and operation of dams that exist; what should be maximized, water for irrigation, production of power through hydroelectric generation, or instream water flows for fish and wildlife values?

Department of Transportation
    The Department of Transportation's primary effect on the landscape

is through the funding that it grants to the states to build the transportation infrastructure. The primary decisions are made at the state level, however, all of them must be approved by the Department of Transportation before a project can go forward. The classic examples of this, which have involved enormous amounts of litigation over the past 20 years, are highway size and siting, and airport planning and expansion.

There are, needless to say, many other management activities engaged in by other federal government departments, but the above list includes all of the major actors and should give an impression of the scope of federal activity in this area.

19.3 REGULATORY ACTIVITIES

Department of Agriculture
   The Department of Agriculture is involved in regulatory activities through its Food Safety Inspection Program, which administers the Meat Safety Act, the Milk Safety Act, the Egg Safety Act, etc. The Department of Agriculture is also involved in recommendations to the Environmental Protection Agency regarding pesticides and to the Department of Labor regulating farmworker conditions, particularly with regard to chemical exposures.

Department of Commerce

* National Oceanographic and Atmospheric Administration (NOAA)
   NOAA, known to most of us primarily through the Weather Bureau, is the agency that administers some major regulatory statutes. The national Coastal Zone Management Program, which oversees state efforts on the coasts of the oceans and of the Great Lakes, is housed here.
* National Marine Fisheries Service
   This little known agency is responsible for regulating commercial marine fishing in the United States. In addition to setting fishing seasons, size limits, year regulations, etc. under its fisheries responsibilities, it is also responsible for administering the Marine Mammal Protection Act, which is designed to help preserve the worldwide populations of whales, dolphins, seals, etc.

Department of the Interior

* Fish and Wildlife Service
   The Fish and Wildlife Service has primary responsibility for the Endangered Species Act. It is the agency that recommends the inclusion of species on the endangered list and recommends the

protection of their habitat. It is also responsible for drawing up and implementing plans for the "restoration" of a species to health so that it can be removed from the Endangered Species Act list. In addition, the Fish and Wildlife Service is also responsible administratively for setting migratory bird hunting seasons under the Migratory Bird Treaty Act, which we have previously discussed.

- Office of Surface Mining

    Under the Surface Mining Control and Reclamation Act, this part of the department regulates all strip and other surface mining. The objectives are to prevent pollution and to restore the land surface as well as possible.

Department of Labor

The Department of Labor gets involved in environmental issues through its management of the Migrant Farm Labor Act. Under this act the department, in conjunction with the Department of Agriculture, sets the standards and the criteria for pesticide exposures to farm labor and, thus, has considerable influence on the rate, manner, and timing of pesticide applications.

Coast Guard

Part of the Department of the Treasury, the Coast Guard has enforcement responsibility for oil spills in U.S. waters.

Corps of Engineers

Under the Water Act, the Corps shares with EPA the duty of designating and protecting wetlands. In addition, under an 1899 statute it can sue to penalize spills into the water.

Council on Environmental Quality (CEQ)

The primary role of CEQ as envisioned in the National Environmental Policy Act (NEPA) that created it is to serve the same role on behalf of the environment that the Council of Economic Advisors serves on behalf of the economy. By executive order it is also responsible for regulating how other federal agencies comply with NEPA.

Food and Drug Administration (FDA)

In conjunction with the Environmental Protection Agency (EPA), the FDA sets the standards for pesticide residues in food.

Nuclear Regulatory Commission (NRC)

The NRC, of course, is responsible for regulating the production, use, and disposal of nuclear materials and licensing the facilities that engage in these activities. With nuclear power plants currently not in high demand, the major environmental problem facing the NRC appears to be the "rear-end" issue of the disposal of radioactive waste. The NRC is responsible for licensing both high-level and low-level radioactive waste disposal sites.

Finally, but not least, we come to the EPA. To discuss the individual statutes and programs of the EPA would require a very large book; in fact, it would require the organizational manual of the agency. Therefore, we shall here do nothing more than list the many statutes for which the EPA has primary responsibility and provide a brief discussion.

- Clean Air Act
- Clean Water Act
- Federal Insecticide, Fungicide and Rodenticide Act
- Safe Drinking Water Act
- Comprehensive Environmental Response Liability and Compensation Act, as amended by the Superfund Amendments and Reauthorization Act
- Resource Conservation and Recovery Act

All of the above statutes can be said to work in roughly the same way. The EPA adopts regulations (pursuant to the Administrative Procedures Act) under which it can delegate its enforcement authority to any state that can demonstrate the ability to properly enforce the standards. If a state comes forward and convinces the EPA that it meets these criteria, then the EPA gives the state the primary responsibility for enforcing the statute. If a state fails to come forward with a plan that the EPA believes will meet the criteria of the federal statute, then the EPA has the responsibility to enforce the federal statute in that state itself.

- Toxic Substances Control Act (TSCA)

   The Toxic Substance Control Act is different from the previously mentioned statutes that EPA enforces. TSCA is really modeled after the FDCA; by this is meant that it is really a system of licensing new chemical compounds before they can be sold in commerce, just as the FDCA is a system for licensing drugs and food additives before they can be sold in commerce. Indeed, just like the FDCA, TSCA has a list of substances, called the *inventory*, which were in use in the United States at the time the act was passed, and, once a substance is on this list, it is up to EPA to prove that the substance is dangerous in order to ban it. With substances not on the inventory, it is up to the proposed manufacturer to prove that the substance is safe before it can be marketed.

- Marine Protection, Research & Sanctuaries Act

   This is the EPA-administered statute that regulates offshore dumping of garbage and other waste materials.

19.4 THE PROBLEM OF CROSS-MEDIA POLLUTION

In my opinion the major problem in environmental law at the moment is that of cross-media conflicts. Under each of the media-based statutes (air, surface water, groundwater, land), EPA sets definite standards that must be met. None of these statutes allows for trade-offs among the various media. In other words, a manufacturing plant must meet the air standards, the water standards, the groundwater standards, and the land disposal standards. No provision is made for even slightly loosening up one of these standards in order to prevent a major problem in one of the other media.

20

Water Law

Having recently co-authored a major monograph on this subject, the author does not really feel ready to tackle it again. Therefore the discussion here will be quite brief, and readers who are interested in more details can refer to that recent monograph.[1]

20.1 RIPARIAN RIGHTS

The riparian system of water law is that which was inherited by the United States from England. The basic principles of riparian law are that any land owner whose property abuts a body of water (that is the meaning of *riparian*) has the right to make any reasonable use of the water. Reasonable, in this context, means that the use does not interfere with other riparians' own use of the water.

In the United States, if a stream is navigable then the public has the right of "navigation" up and down the stream. The definition of navigability varies from jurisdiction to jurisdiction (state to state), but the federal definition of navigability is far and away the most expansive. Basically, it states that if a stream has ever been used for the transport of people or goods or, with the expenditure of a not unreasonable amount of money could be made suitable for the transport of people or goods, then it is navigable.[2]

As long as a riparian's use of the water does not unreasonably interfere with other riparians' uses of the water, then it is permitted. An example of a use that would interfere would be to withdraw all of the water from the stream, for irrigation or other use, leaving people downstream with no water whatsoever.

20.2 APPROPRIATION SYSTEMS

The other major system of water law in the United States is called the appropriation system. It is a U.S. development and owes its origins to the unsuitability of riparian law to the conditions found by settlers when they got west of the hundredth meridian. This is an area of limited water and many of the streams dry up during the summer; thus there were continual disputes as to who could use the water.

All of us, I suspect, have seen old cowboy movies in which the bad guy is trying to buy up all of the water rights in the valley. This is what the appropriations system is about. A person gets the right to use water, and this right can be transferred from individual to individual. Unlike the right to use water under a riparian system, an owner of an appropriation permit does not have to own land along the water course. The permits are granted by a state official, whatever the title might be, and are registered in the official records. If there is a water shortage, the water permit holder with the oldest permit gets to fulfill all of his or her needs before anyone else can take any water; then the permit holder with the second oldest permit gets to fulfill all of his needs, etc.; the end result is that the newest permit holders get no water at all in water shortage years. This is what is meant by "first in time, first in right."

This might, at first glance, appear either harsh or irrational, but it is not. What it means is that, instead of spreading the loss of a water shortage across all of the individuals who depend on that water, we will let a few of them continue to operate in their normal manner and penalize those who are newcomers. In some instances, then, a water permit can be more valuable than the land on which the water is used. This is, in fact, a not uncommon situation, and for those who remember the movie "Chinatown," the fight there was about the cities buying the water permits from farmers on marginal land who really had no use for them.

20.3 HYBRID SYSTEMS

The most recent development in U.S. water law is that of hybrid water law systems. Under a hybrid system a water user needs to get a permit, but all permits of equal date are treated equally, and all users of water on the date the system is instituted are granted permits for the total amount of water they are currently using.

The virtue that some riparian states see in adopting a hybrid permit system is that it will enable the state to get an exact measure of how much water is currently being used by all users, and that it will also keep any water fights that might occur out of the courts and have them resolved by an administrative agency. There is, admittedly, considerable merit in keeping disputes out of court. Courts take a long time to resolve almost any issue. Despite this, however, it was the author's judgment in a monograph written a year ago, that Michigan, for example, had nothing to gain from adopting a hybrid water law system; the transaction costs of making the switch more than outweighed the benefits that might follow from it.

REFERENCES

1. Bronstein, D. A., Fitch, E. J., Larsen, L. D., and Leighty, L. L., Hybrid Water Law Systems: Would one be Advantageous for Michigan?, Michigan Sea Grant Report # MICHU-SG-89-200 (1989).
2. *U.S. v. Appalachian Power Co., 311 U.S. 377 (1940).*

21

Other Legal Matters

21.1 INTELLECTUAL PROPERTY — PATENTS, COPYRIGHTS, TRADEMARKS

Under the Constitution, Congress was told to create a system of promoting and protecting inventors and authors, i.e., establishing a system of patents and copyrights. This, of course, has been done. As I am not an expert on any of these areas of law, I will only make a few brief comments about them. Patents are granted for advancement of knowledge in the "useful arts." One of the requirements for the granting of a patent is that an actual working piece of equipment, or, at least, a model of it, have been achieved; this is the *reduced to practice* requirement.

A patent application is a public record, and when the life of the patent monopoly expires, other that are fully entitled to use the knowledge which is contained in the patent. This is the whole reason behind the patent system: to advance the state of the art, but, at the same time, give a reward to the originator of the concept by granting a monopoly for a limited period of time. Most court fights concerning patents deal with the question of whether the patent should have been granted in the first place. The primary issue, as I as an outsider read the cases, appears to be whether the learning reflected in the patent is a significant advancement over "the prior art."

Copyrights protect the specific expression of an idea; they do not protect the idea itself. It is impossible, in other words, to secure legal protection for the concept behind a piece of writing, a piece of art, etc. Only the specific expression in a given instance can be protected.

A trademark is registered in order to prevent other people from, in affect, "misbranding" the origin of a particular item. Only the holder of the trademark has the right to mark goods with that symbol or name, and thus if one buys something with that symbol or name on it, one is supposed to be sure that it came from the expected source. Unlike patents and copyrights, which expire after a specified period of time, a trademark is good for as long as it is in continuous use.

21.2 TRADE SECRETS

Since a patent will, by its own terms, expire at some future date, many advancements in the "state of the art" are never patented. Instead the developers of these advancements keep their information secret to prevent other parties from learning it, and thus can use it, exclusively, as long as nobody learns the secret. The only legal protection that a trade secret receives is that contracts requiring that one party not disclose trade secrets learned from the other party are enforceable, both by money damages for breech and by injunction to prevent prospective breech. Thus, if one has a truly revolutionary method of manufacturing a common item (e.g., an automobile tire or a pencil), one might do best to just secure trade secret protection of the process. On the other hand, if one invents the Polaroid™* camera or the process of xerography, patent protection is probably the most useful thing. This is because a new and revolutionary product that does not have patent protection can be reversed engineered by competitors and duplicated freely, as it has only trade secret protection, which is good only as long as the secret can be kept.

21.3 "BUSINESS" OR "COMMERCIAL" LAW

"Business" or "commercial" law has been codified in the United States in the past 40 years as the states have adopted what is called the Uniform Commercial Code (UCC). The UCC sets forth how contracts are formed between parties of roughly equal bargaining power, how they shall be interpreted and enforced, etc. It also deals with such things as negotiable instruments (checks, bearer bonds, etc.), letters of credit, and similar items. This is an area in which I have learned nothing since my days in law school and can only suggest that those interested refer to one of the many treatises on these subjects.

21.4 INTERNATIONAL LAW

Being something of a cynic myself, it is still my fundamental belief that the basic principle of international law is "might makes right." The only international law that is enforceable is that which is specified by treaty, and even there, only between private individuals subject to the

---

* Registered trademark of the Polaroid Company.

treaty, not between the contracting states who are the parties to the treaties. There is no way to force another country to live up to obligations it has assumed under a treaty, except to institute a commercial embargo, go to war, etc.

This is not to say, however, that treaties are worthless or that international agreements and accords should not be entered into. If nothing else, they can provide a standard against which the actions of states can be measured. This is probably best exemplified by the Helsinki Accords on Human Rights, which were adopted in the 1970s by many states (including the Soviet Union) and set forth what are believed to be the basic standards of state conduct towards individuals. In the same tradition, I am currently part of a committee that is attempting to draft a set of accords regarding intergenerational environmental rights.

All that said, however, the fact is that, in my opinion, international law is really a matter of politics, not of law.

21.5 LOCAL GOVERNMENT LAW

Local government law, of course, varies very much from state to state. The only really fundamental thing that can be said to be true almost universally about local government law is that local government agencies have only those powers that the state allows them. A county, city, township, etc. does not have any inherent powers; it only has the right to exercise those powers that the state, by passing a statute, grants to it. Those interested in finding out the details of local government law in their state might well be referred to the cooperative extension service of their land grant university, which probably has some bulletins and other publications regarding local government in that state.

21.6 THE BOSS IS LIABLE — *RESPONDEAT SUPERIOR*

This is the Latin legal term for the principle that a superior is responsible for the activities of subordinates if those actions are taken within the course of the subordinate's functions. Under this doctrine, if I am driving my car on my employer's business and have a collision, not only am I potentially liable, but so is my employer.

The basic idea is that corporations and other large organizations do not take actions themselves — they only act through agents. If the agent is pursuing the employer's ends for the employer's benefit, then the employer is potentially liable for the agent's acts. Most fights about the application of *respondeat superior* arise from deciding whether the act was taken "in the course of employment." If it was then the doctrine applies; if it was not then the doctrine does not apply. The case in which *respondeat superior* does not apply is that of the agent acting *ultra vires*, a term we discussed in connection with sovereign immunity. If the act is outside the agent's authority, then it is *ultra vires* and *respondeat superior* does not apply.

Appendix A

How to Find It — The Basics of Legal Citation

A typical legal citation to a court decision might look like this: *Brown v. Laitner*, 435 N.W. 2d 1 (Mich. 1989).

This is broken down as follows:

- *Brown v. Laitner* is the name of the case;
- 435 is the number of the volume in which the case is found;
- *N.W. 2d* is the abbreviated name of the set to which the volume belongs;
- 1 is the page of that volume where the case begins;
- *Mich.* is the abbreviation for the court that decided the case; and
- *1989* is the year in which it was decided.

In this particular example, *N.W. 2d* refers to the Northwestern Reporter, Second Series and *Mich.* indicates it was decided by the Michigan Supreme Court.

Another example: *Stop H-3 Ass'n v. Dole* 870 F. 2d 1419 (9th Cir. 1989). This case was decided by the United States Court of Appeals for the Ninth Circuit in 1989 and is found on page 1419 of volume 870 of the *Federal Reporter*, Second Series.

For a statute the citation might look like this: 42 U.S.C. [A.] 4321 (1989).

This breaks down as:

- *42* is Title 42;
- *U.S.C.* is United States Code (if *A.*, United States Code Annotated);
- *4321* is Section 4321; and
- *1989* is the date of the volume referenced (not the date of enactment).

123

This happens to be the citation of the National Environmental Policy Act (NEPA)of 1970.

Legal journals are cited the same way: Bronstein, State Regulation of Powerplant Siting, 3 *Environmental Law* 273 (1973) appeared in volume 3 of the journal *Environmental Law* in 1973 and started at page 273.

Lawyers cite **all** journals, legal or not, this way: Bronstein, Some Ethical Issues in Toxicology, 7 *Fund. App. Tox.* 525 (1986) appeared in volume 7 of *Fundamental & Applied Toxicology* starting at page 525 in 1986.

Legal citations also include the history of a case. For example, in the discussion of the concept of standing in Chapter 7 is the citation:

Velvel v. Johnson, 287 F. Supp. 846 (D. Kan. 1968); aff'd. sub nom *Velvel v. Nixon*, 415 F. 2d 236 (10 Cir 1969), cert. denied 396 U.S. 1042 (1970).

Here the original suit was decided in Kansas in 1968 involving President Johnson and the District Court opinion is found in volume 287 of *Federal Supplement* at page 846. The decision was appealed and affirmed by the 10th Circuit in 1969 but, since the President was now Nixon, the name of the case changed and that decision can be found in volume 415 of the *Federal Reporter* at page 236. The 1970 order of the Supreme Court denying the writ of *certiorari* (see Chapter 2) is then found in volume 396 of the *United States Reports* at page 1042.

The absolutely necessary reference to the abbreviations that appear in legal citations is *A Uniform System of Citation*, published by the *Harvard Law Review* and commonly referred to as the *blue book*. If you believe that you might ever have to look something up in a law library, you should have a copy of the blue book. What follows is a summary reference to some of the most common legal citations and sources.

THE NATIONAL REPORTER SYSTEM

West Publishing Company publishes what is called the *National Reporter System*. It is a collection of sets of volumes having the cases of various courts in each set.

State Regional Reporters

Atl. and A. 2d — Atlantic Reporter: Connecticut, Delaware, Maine, Maryland, New Hampshire, New Jersey, Pennsylvania, Rhode Island, Vermont, District of Columbia Municipal Court of Appeals.

N.E. and N.E. 2d — North Eastern Reporter: Illinois, Indiana, Massachusetts, New York, Ohio.

N.W. and N.W. 2d — North Western Reporter: Iowa, Michigan, Minnesota, Nebraska, North Dakota, South Dakota, Wisconsin.

Pac. and P. 2d — Pacific Reporter: Alaska, Arizona, California, Colorado, Hawaii, Idaho, Kansas, Montana, Nevada, New Mexico, Oklahoma, Oregon, Utah, Washington, Wyoming.

S.E. and S.E. 2d — South Eastern Reporter: Georgia, North Carolina, South Carolina, Virginia, West Virginia.

S.W. and S.W. 2d — South Western Reporter: Arkansas, Kentucky, Missouri, Tennessee, Texas.

Sou. and S. 2d — Southern Reporter: Alabama, Florida, Louisiana, Mississippi.

Federal Reporters

Fed. and F. 2d — Federal Reporter: All federal intermediate appellate and specialized appeals courts.

F. Supp. — Federal Supplement: All federal district courts and the Customs Court.

F.R.D. — Federal Rules Decisions: All federal district court decisions that discuss the Federal Rules of Civil Procedure or the Federal Rules of Criminal Procedure.

THE SUPREME COURT

There are four common ways in which the decisions of the Supreme Court are cited, and each has a different reason for existence:

U.S.

This is the official version of the decisions, published by the Government Printing Office. It is always included in a citation to a Supreme Court decision, even if the case being cited has not yet appeared in it. The problem with it is that it has the greatest time lag between the issuance of the opinion and the appearance of the volume.

U.S.L.W. or L.W. — U.S. Law Week

This is published by the Bureau of National Affairs and is the first version of a Supreme Court opinion to appear in print. As a normal matter there is at most a 10-day delay between the issuance of an opinion and its appearance here. This is where to go to find the text of a decision you have recently read about in the newspaper. It contains only the full text of the opinion, with no summary or other information.

S. Ct. — Supreme Court Reporter

This is the West Publishing Company *National Reporter System* set that publishes Supreme Court decisions. It includes a summary description of the case from West's editors and the official syllabus of the decision from the Clerk's office. The time delay is generally four to six weeks.

L.Ed. and L. Ed. 2d — Lawyers Edition

Published by Lawyers Co-operative, this includes summaries of the briefs filed by each side and a resumé of the oral arguments presented by the lawyers. Thus it is very useful for research, as you can learn what questions the Supreme Court avoided answering in its decision as well as what was actually decided.

Citation Etiquette

The following ways of citing the imaginary Supreme Court case of Smith v. Jones would all be acceptable:

Smith v. Jones, U.S. , 37 L.W. 1258 (1990) if the case has only appeared in *Law Week* at the time of writing. (Notice the U.S. .)

Smith v. Jones, U.S. , 110 S. Ct. 1254, L. Ed. 2d (1990) if the *Lawyers Edition* version has not yet appeared. (If it has, then the blanks are filled in appropriately.)

Once the official version has appeared both of the following are acceptable:

Smith v. Jones, 435 U.S. 267 (1990)

Smith v. Jones, 435 U.S. 267, 110 S. Ct. 1254, 45 L. Ed 2d 890 (1990).

The point is that if one mentions either of the unofficial reporters, one must mention both of them.

SPECIALIZED REPORTERS

There are all sorts of specialized reporters that attempt to gather all cases on a given subject into one set. The one I use the most, for example, is abbreviated Env't. Rep. Cas. for *Environment Reporter — Cases.* Env't. Rep. Cas. is published weekly by the Bureau of National Affairs and purports to include all reported court decisions involving environmental issues, both state and federal. Almost any field of law one can imagine has such a specialized service, from abortions (Abortion L. Rep.) through workers compensation (Workmen's Comp. L. Rep.).

SHEPARD'S CITATIONS

In order to determine the previous and subsequent history of a case, a lawyer resorts to a set known as *Shepard's Citations.* This set of volumes gives cross-references to the history of a given case and also lists every subsequent case that has cited that case. Thus to determine whether a principle stated in a given case has subsequently changed, one Shepardizes the original citation to see if it is changed by later cases.

COMMENTARIES ON THE LAW

If one wants to find a discussion on the current state of the law on a given subject, or to learn the fundamentals of a particular legal area, there are several possible approaches. They are discussed here in the order in which I use them when necessary; that does not mean that you might not wish to go through them in some other order.

Law Reviews

Law is a somewhat unique field in that many of the professional journals for lawyers are edited by law students. Thus it is a case of the students deciding what the practitioners should read. The *Harvard Law Review* is edited by third-year students at Harvard Law School; it is as though the *New England Journal of Medicine* were edited by fourth-year students at Harvard Medical School.

The articles in law reviews are written by professors and practicing lawyers and, despite my comments above, the student editors generally do an excellent job in deciding what to publish. One finds law review articles on the topic one is interested in by consulting the *Index to Legal Periodicals* or a similar reference; they are the legal equivalents of the *Reader's Guide to Periodical Literature*.

Treatises

Almost any field of law has one or more treatises written about it. These are one- or more-volume works discussing all aspects of the field. Needless to say, they are, again, written by professors or practicing lawyers, but they are issued by commercial publishers and edited by them. Treatises should not be taken blindly on faith; sometimes they are written from a particular point of view and sometimes they are out of date. Before relying on a treatise, one should do a bit of checking by reading some of the cases the author cites as supporting a point and deciding if they really do.

Annotated Cases

Lawyers Co-operative (the publishers of *Lawyers Edition*) also issues sets that consist of a case on a particular subject followed by a discussion (many are over 100 pages long) of the issue in the case. These are referred to, collectively, as A.L.R., for the original set, *American Law Reports*. Nowadays there are several such sets; A.L.R., A.L.R. 2d, A.L.R. 3d, A.L.R. Fed., etc. The comments are written by staff lawyers at the publisher and are generally accurate statements of the existing law. The main drawback is the lack of opinion and of attempts to predict where the law in the area might be headed.

Legal Encyclopedias

There are two competing legal encyclopedias; C.J.S. (*Corpus Juris Secundum*) from West Publishing Company, and Am. Jur. (*American Jurisprudence*) from Lawyers Co-operative. They are exactly what I've called them, encyclopedias. Thus they suffer from the standard problem of that type of work, lack of depth in the discussion. Personally, I only use Am. Jur., and then only as a source of references to A.L.R. You, however, might find them more useful.

Appendix B

Extracts from the Federal Rules of Civil Procedure

Rule 3. Commencement of Action

A civil action is commenced by filing a complaint with the court.

Rule 7. Pleadings Allowed; Form of Motions

(a) Pleadings. There shall be a complaint and an answer; a reply to a counterclaim denominated as such; an answer to a cross-claim, if the answer contains a cross-claim; a third-party complaint, if a person who was not an original party is summoned ...; and a third-party answer, if a third-party complaint is served. No other pleading shall be allowed, except that the court may order a reply to an answer or a third-party answer.

Rule 8. General Rules of Pleading

(a) Claims for Relief. A pleading which sets forth a claim for relief, whether an original claim, counterclaim, cross-claim, or third-party claim, shall contain (1) a short and plain statement of the grounds upon which the court's jurisdiction depends, unless the court already has jurisdiction and the claim needs no new grounds of jurisdiction to support it, (2) a short and plain statement of the claim showing that the pleader is entitled to relief, and (3) a demand for judgment for the relief the pleader seeks. Relief in the alternative or of several different types may be demanded.

(b) Defenses; Form of Denials. A party shall state in short and plain terms the party's defenses to each claim asserted and shall admit or deny the averments upon which the adverse party relies. If a party is without knowledge or information sufficient to form a belief as to the truth of an averment, the party shall so state and this has the effect of a denial. Denials shall fairly meet the substance of the averments denied. When a pleader intends in good faith to deny only a part or a qualification of an averment, the pleader shall specify so much of it as is true and material and shall deny only the remainder. Unless the pleader intends in good faith to controvert all the averments of the preceding pleading, the pleader may make denials as specific denials of designated averments or paragraphs or may generally deny all the averments except such designated averments or paragraphs as the pleader expressly admits; but, when the pleader does so intend to controvert all its averments, including averments of the grounds upon which the court's jurisdiction depends, the pleader may do so by general denial ... .

(c) **Affirmative Defenses.** In pleading to a preceding pleading, a party shall set forth affirmatively accord and satisfaction, arbitration and award, assumption of risk, contributory negligence, discharge in bankruptcy, duress, estoppel, failure of consideration, fraud, illegality, injury by fellow servant, laches, license, payment, release, res judicata, statute of frauds, statute of limitations, waiver, and any other matter constituting an avoidance or affirmative defense. When a party has mistakenly designated a defense as a counterclaim or a counterclaim as a defense, the court on terms, if justice so requires, shall treat the pleading as if there had been a proper designation.

(d) **Effect of Failure to Deny.** Averments in a pleading to which a responsive pleading is required, other than those as to the amount of damage, are admitted when not denied in the responsive pleading. Averments in a pleading to which no responsive pleading is required or permitted shall be taken as denied or avoided.

(e) **Pleading to be Concise and Direct; Consistency.** (1) Each averment of a pleading shall be simple, concise, and direct. No technical forms of pleading or motions are required. (2) A party may set forth two or more statements of a claim or defense alternately or hypothetically, either in one count or defense or in separate counts or defenses. When two or more statements are made in the alternative and one of them if made independently would be sufficient, the pleading is not made insufficient by the insufficiency of one or more of the alternative statements. A party may also state as many separate claims or defenses as the party has regardless of consistency and whether based on legal, equitable, or maritime grounds ... .

(f) **Construction of Pleadings**. All pleadings shall be so construed as to do substantial justice.

Rule 9. Pleading Special Matters

(a) **Capacity.** It is not necessary to aver the capacity of a party to sue or be sued or the authority of a party to sue or be sued ... except to the extent required to show the jurisdiction of the court. When a party desires to raise an issue as to the legal existence of any party or the capacity of any party to sue or be sued or the authority of a party to sue or be sued in a representative capacity, the party desiring to raise the issue shall do so by specific negative averment, which shall include such supporting particulars as are peculiarly within the pleader's knowledge.

(b) Fraud, Mistake, Condition of the Mind. In all averments of fraud or mistake, the circumstances constituting fraud or mistake shall be stated with particularity. Malice, intent, knowledge, and other condition of mind of a person may be averred generally.

(c) Conditions Precedent. In pleading the performance or occurrence of conditions precedent, it is sufficient to aver generally that all conditions precedent have been performed or have occurred. A denial of performance or occurrence shall be made specifically and with particularity.

(d) Official Document or Act. In pleading an official document or official act it is sufficient to aver that the document was issued or the act done in compliance with law.

(e) Judgment. In pleading a judgment or decision of a domestic or foreign court, judicial or quasijudicial tribunal, or of a board or officer it is sufficient to aver the judgment or decision without setting forth matter showing jurisdiction to render it.

(f) Time and Place. For the purpose of testing the sufficiency of a pleading, averments of time and place are material and shall be considered like all other averments of material matter.

(g) Special Damage. When items of special damage are claimed, they shall be specifically stated.

Rule 12. Defenses and Objections — When and How Presented — By Pleading or Motion — Motion for Judgment on the pleadings

(a) When Presented. A defendant shall serve an answer within 20 days after the service of the summons and complaint upon that defendant.... A party served with a pleading stating a cross-claim against that party shall serve an answer thereto within 20 days after the service upon that party. The plaintiff shall serve a reply to a counterclaim in the answer within 20 days after service of the answer, or, if a reply is ordered by the court, within 20 days after service of the order, unless the order otherwise directs. The United States or an officer or agency thereof shall serve an answer to the complaint or to a cross-claim, or a reply to a counterclaim, within 50 days after the service upon the United States attorney of the pleading in which the claim is asserted. The service of a motion permitted under this rule alters these periods of time as follows, unless a different time is fixed by order of the court: (1) if the court denies the motion or postpones its disposition until the trial on the merits, the responsive pleading shall be served within 10 days after notice of the court's action; (2) if the court grants a motion for a more definite statement the responsive pleading shall be served within 10 days after the service of the more definite statement.

(b) **How presented.** Every defense, in law or fact, to a claim for relief in any pleading, whether a claim, counterclaim, cross-claim, or third-party claim, shall be asserted in the responsive pleading thereto if one is required, except that the following defenses may at the option of the pleader by made by motion: (1) lack of jurisdiction over the subject matter, (2) lack of jurisdiction over the person, (3) improper venue, (4) insufficiency of process, (5) insufficiency of service of process, (6) failure to state a claim upon which relief can be granted, (7) failure to join a party ... . A motion making any of these defenses shall be made before pleading if a further pleading is permitted. No defense or objection is waived by being joined with one or more other defenses or objections in a responsive pleading or motion. If a pleading sets forth a claim for relief to which the adverse party is not required to serve a responsive pleading, the adverse party may assert at the trial any defense in law or fact to that claim for relief. If, on a motion asserting the defense numbered (6) to dismiss for a failure of the pleading to state a claim upon which relief can be granted, matters outside the pleading are presented to and not excluded by the court, the motion shall be treated as one for summary judgment and disposed of as provided in Rule 56, and all parties shall be given reasonable opportunity to present all material made pertinent to such a motion by Rule 56.

(c) **Motion for Judgment on the Pleadings**. After the pleadings are closed but within such time as not to delay the trial, any party may move for judgment on the pleadings. If, on a motion for judgment on the pleadings, matters outside the pleadings are presented to and not excluded by the court, the motion shall be treated as one for summary judgment and disposed of as provided in Rule 56, and all parties shall be given reasonable opportunity to present all material made pertinent to such a motion by Rule 56.

(d) **Preliminary Hearings.** The defenses specifically enumerated (1) — (7) in subdivision (b) of this rule, whether made in a pleading or by motion, and the motion for judgment mentioned in subdivision (c) of this rule shall be heard and determined before trial on application of any party, unless the court orders that the hearing and determination thereof be deferred until the trial.

(e) **Motion for More Definite Statement.** If a pleading to which a responsive pleading is permitted is so vague or ambiguous that a party cannot reasonably be required to frame a responsive pleading, the party may move for a more definite statement before interposing a responsive pleading. The motion shall point out the defects complained of and the details desired. If the motion is granted and the order of the court is not obeyed within 10 days after notice of the order or within such other time as the court may fix, the court may strike the pleading to which the motion was directed or make such order as it deems just.

(f) **Motion to Strike.** Upon motion made by a party before respond-ing to a pleading or, if no responsive pleading is permitted by these rules, upon motion made by a party within 20 days after the service of the pleading upon the party or upon the court's own initiative at any time, the court may order stricken from any pleading any insufficient defense or any redundant, immaterial, impertinent, or scandalous matter.

(g) **Consolidation of Defenses in Motion.** A party who makes a motion under this rule may join with it any other motions herein provided for and then available to the party. If a party makes a motion under this rule but omits therefrom any defense or objection then available to the party which this rule permits to be raised by motion, the party shall not thereafter make a motion based on the defense or objection so omitted, except a motion as provided in subdivision (h) (2) hereof on any of the grounds there stated.

(h) **Waiver or Preservation of Certain Defenses.** (1) A defense of lack of jurisdiction over the person, improper venue, insufficiency of proc-ess, or insufficiency of service of process is waived (A) if omitted from a motion in the circumstances described in subdivision (g), or (B) if it is neither made by motion under this rule nor included in a responsive pleading or an amendment thereof permitted by Rule 15 (a) to be made as a matter of course. (2) A defense of failure to state a claim upon which relief can be granted, a defense of failure to join a party indispensable under Rule 19, and an objection of failure to state a legal defense to a claim may be made in any pleading permitted or ordered under Rule 7(a), or by motion for judgment on the pleadings, or at the trial on the merits. (3) Whenever it appears by suggestion of the parties or other-wise that the court lacks jurisdiction of the subject matter, the court shall dismiss the action.

Rule 13. Counterclaim and Cross-Claim

(a) **Compulsory Counterclaims.** A pleading shall state as a counter-claim any claim which at the time of serving the pleading the pleader has against any opposing party, if it arises out of the transaction or occurrence that is the subject matter of the opposing party's claim and does not require for its adjudication the presence of third parties of whom the court cannot acquire jurisdiction. But the pleader need not state the claim if (1) at the time the action was commenced the claim was the subject of another pending action, or (2) the opposing party brought suit upon the claim by attachment or other process by which the court did not acquire jurisdiction to render a personal judgment on the claim, and the pleader is not stating any counterclaim under this Rule 13.

(b) Permissive Counterclaims. A pleading may state as a counterclaim any claim against an opposing party not arising out of the transaction or occurrence that is the subject matter of the opposing party's claim.

(c) Counterclaim Exceeding Opposing Claim. A counterclaim may or may not diminish or defeat the recovery sought by the opposing party. It may claim relief exceeding in amount or different in kind from that sought in the pleading of the opposing party.

(d) Counterclaim against the U.S. These rules shall not be construed to enlarge beyond the limits now fixed by law the right to assert counterclaims or to claim credits against the United States or an officer or agency thereof.

(e) Counterclaim Maturing or Acquired After Pleading. A claim which either matured or was acquired by the pleader after serving a pleading may, with the permission of the court, be presented as a counterclaim by supplemental pleading.

(f) Omitted Counterclaim. When a pleader fails to set up a counterclaim through oversight, inadvertence, or excusable neglect, or when justice requires, the pleader may by leave of court set up the counterclaim by amendment.

(g) Cross-Claim Against Co-Party. A pleading may state as a cross-claim any claim by one party against a co-party arising out of the transaction or occurrence that is the subject matter either of the original action or of a counterclaim therein or relating to any property that is the subject matter of the original action. Such cross-claim may include a claim that the party against whom it is asserted is or may be liable to the cross-claimant for all or part of a claim asserted in the action against the cross-claimant.

(h) Joinder of Additional Parties. Persons other than those made parties to the original action may be made parties to a counterclaim or cross-claim in accordance with the provisions of Rules 19 and 20.

(i) Separate Trials; Separate Judgments. If the court orders separate trials as provided in [these rules], judgment on a counterclaim or cross-claim may be rendered in accordance with the terms of Rule 54(b) when the court has jurisdiction so to do, even if the claims of the opposing party have been dismissed or otherwise disposed of.

Rule 16. Pre-Trial Conferences; Scheduling; Management

(a) Pretrial Conferences; Objectives.
In any action, the court may in its discretion direct the attorneys for the parties and any unrepresented parties to appear before it for a confer-

ence or conferences before trial for such purposes as (1) expediting the disposition of the action; (2) establishing early and continuing control so that the case will not be protracted because of lack of management; (3) discouraging wasteful pretrial activities; (4) improving the quality of the trial through more thorough preparation, and; (5) facilitating the settlement of the case.

(b) Scheduling and Planning. Except in categories of actions exempted by district court rule [the court] shall, after consulting with the attorneys for the parties and any unrepresented parties, by a scheduling conference, telephone, mail, or other suitable means, enter a scheduling order that limits the time (1) to join other parties and to amend the pleadings: (2) to file and hear motions; and (3) to complete discovery. The schduling order also may include (4) the date or dates for conferences before trial, a final pretrial conference, and trial; and (5) any other matters appropriate in the circumstances of the case. The order shall issue as soon as practicable but in no event more than 120 days after filing of the complaint. A schedule shall not be modified except by leave of the judge or a magistrate when authorized by district court rule upon a showing of good cause.

(c) Subjects to be Discussed at Pretrial Conferences. The participants at any conference under this rule may consider and take action with respect to (1) the formulation and simplification of the issues, including the elimination of frivolous claims or defenses; (2) the necessity or desirability of amendments to the pleadings; (3) documents which will avoid unnecessary proof, stipulations regarding the authenticity of documents, and advance rulings from the court on the admissibility of evidence; (4) the avoidance of unnecessary proof and of cumulative evidence; (5) the identification of witnesses and documents, the need and schedule for filing and exchanging pretrail briefs, and the date or dates for further conferences and for trial; (6) the advisability of referring matters to a magistrate or master; (7) the possibility of settlement or the use of extrajudicial procedures to resolve the dispute; (8) the form and substance of the pretrial order; (9) the disposition of pending motions; (10) the need for adopting special procedures for managing potentially difficult or protracted actions that may involve complex issues, multiple parties, difficult legal questions, or unusual proof problems; and (11) such other matters as may aid in the disposition of the action. At least one of the attorneys for each party participating in any conference before trial shall have authority to enter into stipulations and to make admissions regarding all matters that the participants may reasonably anticipate may be discussed.

(d) Final Pretrial Conference. Any final pretrial conference shall be held as close to the time of trial as reasonable under the circumstances. The participants at any such conference shall formulate a plan for trial, including a program for facilitating the admission of evidence. The conference shall be attended by at least one of the attorneys who will conduct the trial for each of the parties and by any unrepresented parties.

(e) Pretrial Orders. After any conference held pursuant to this rule, an order shall be entered reciting the action taken. This order shall control the subsequent course of the action unless modified by a subsequent order. The order following a final pretrial conference shall be modified only to prevent manifest injustice.

Rule 23. Class Actions

(a) Prerequisites to a Class Action. One or more members of a class may sue or be sued as representative parties on behalf of all only if (1) the class is so numerous that joinder of all members is impracticable, (2) there are questions of law or fact common to the class, (3) the claims or defenses of the representative parties are typical of the claims or defenses of the class, and (4) the representative parties will fairly and adequately protect the interests of the class.

(b) Class Actions Maintainable. An action may be maintained as a class action if the prerequisites of subdivision (a) are satisfied, and in addition: (1) the prosecution of separate actions by or against individual members of the class would create a risk of (A) inconsistent or varying adjudications with respect to individual members of the class which would establish incompatible standards of conduct for the party opposing the class, or (B) adjudications with respect to individual members of the class which would as a practical matter be dispositive of the interests of the other members not parties to the adjudications or substantially impair or impede their ability to protect their interests; or (2) the party opposing the class has acted or refused to act on grounds generally applicable to the class, thereby making appropriate final injunctive relief or corresponding declaratory relief with respect to the class as a whole; or (3) the court finds that the questions of law or fact common to the members of the class predominate over any questions affecting only individual members, and that a class action is superior to other available methods for the fair and efficient adjudication of the controversy. The matters pertinent to the findings include: (A) the interest of members of the class in individually controlling the prosecution or defense of separate actions; (B) the extent and nature of any litigation concerning the controversy already commenced by or against members of the class; (C) the desirability or undesirability of concentrating the litigation of the claims in the particular forum; (D) the difficulties likely to be encountered in the management of a class action.

(c) Determination by Order Whether Class Action to be Maintained; Notice; Judgment; Actions Conducted Partially as Class Actions. (1) As soon as practicable after the commencement of an action brought as a class action, the court shall determine by order whether it is to be so maintained. An order under this subdivision may be conditional, and may be altered or amended before the decision on the merits. (2) In any class action maintained under subdivision (b)(3), the court shall direct to the members of the class the best notice practicable under the circumstances, including individual notice to all members who can be identified through reasonable effort. The notice shall advise each member that (A) the court will exclude the member from the class if the member so requests by specified date; (B) the judgment, whether favorable or not, will include all members who do not request exclusion; and (C) any member who does not request exclusion may, if the member desires, enter an appearance through counsel. (3) The judgment in an action maintained as a class action under subdivision (b)(1) or (b)(2), whether or not favorable to the class, shall include and describe those whom the court finds to be members of the class. The judgment in an action maintained as a class action under subdivision (b)(3), whether or not favorable to the class, shall include and specify or describe those to whom the notice provided in subdivision (c)(2) was directed, and who have not requested exclusion, and whom the court finds to be members of the class. (4) When appropriate (A) an action may be brought or maintained as a class action with respect to particular issues, or (B) a class may be divided into subclasses and each subclass treated as a class, and the provisions of this rule shall then be construed and applied accordingly.

(d) Orders in Conduct of Actions. In the conduct of actions to which this rule applies, the court may make appropriate orders: (1) determining the course of proceedings or prescribing measures to prevent undue repetition or complication in the presentation of evidence or argument; (2) requiring, for the protection of the members of the class or otherwise for the fair conduct of the action, that notice be given in such manner as the court may direct to some or all of the members of any step in the action, or of the proposed extent of the judgment, or of the opportunity of members to signify whether they consider the representation fair and adequate, to intervene and present claims or defenses, or otherwise to come into the action; (3) imposing conditions on the representative parties or on intervenors; (4) requiring that the pleadings be amended to eliminate therefrom allegations as to representation of absent persons, and that the action proceed accordingly; (5) dealing with similar procedural matters. The orders may be combined with an order under Rule 16, and may be altered or amended as may be desirable from time to time.

(e) Dismissal or Compromise. A class action shall not be dismissed or compromised without the approval of the court, and notice of the proposed dismissal or compromise shall be given to all members of the class in such manner as the court directs.

Rule 25. Substitution of Parties

(a) **Death.** (1) If a party dies and the claim is not thereby extinguished, the court may order substitution of the proper parties. The motion for substitution may be made by any party or by the successors or representatives of the deceased party and, together with the notice of hearing, shall be served on the parties as provided in [these rules]. Unless the motion for substitution is made not later than 90 days after the death is suggested upon the record of service of a statement of the fact of the death as provided herein for the service of the motion, the action shall be dismissed as to the deceased party. (2) In the event of the death of one or more of the plaintiffs or of one or more of the defendants in the action in which the right sought to be enforced survives only to the surviving plaintiffs or only against the surviving defendants, the action does not abate. The death shall be suggested upon the record and the action shall proceed in favor of or against the surviving parties.

(b) **Incompetency.** If a party becomes incompetent, the court upon motion served as provided in subdivision (a) of this rule may allow the action to be continued by or against the party's representative.

(c) **Transfer of Interest.** In case of any transfer of interest, the action may be continued by or against the original party, unless the court upon motion directs the person to whom the interest is transferred to be substituted in the action or joined with the original party. Service of the motion shall be made as provided in subdivision (a) of this rule.

(d) **Public Officers; Death or Separation from Office.** (1) When a public officer is a party to an action in an official capacity and during its pendency dies, resigns, or otherwise ceases to hold office, the action does not abate and the officer's successor is automatically substituted as a party. Proceedings following the substitution shall be in the name of the substituted party, but any misnomer not affecting the substantial rights of the parties shall be disregarded. An order of substitution may be entered at any time, but the omission to enter such an order shall not affect the substitution. (2) A public officer who sue or is sued in an official capacity may be described as a party by the officer's official title rather than by name; but the court may require the officer's name to be added.

Rule 26. General Provisions Governing Discovery

(a) **Discovery Methods.** Parties may obtain discovery by one or more of the following methods: depositions upon oral examination or written questions; written interrogatories; production of documents or things or permission to enter upon land or other property, for inspection and other purposes; physical and mental examinations; and requests for admission.

(b) Discovery Scope and Limits. Unless otherwise limited by order of the court in accordance with these rules, the scope of discovery is as follows: (1) In General. Parties may obtain discovery regarding any matter, not privileged, which is relevant to the subject matter involved in the pending action, whether it relates to the claim or defense of the party seeking discovery or to the claim or defense of any other party, including the existence, description, nature, custody, condition and location of any books, documents, or other tangible things and the identify and location of persons having knowledge of any discoverable matter. It is not ground for objection that the information sought will be inadmissible at the trial if the information sought appears reasonably calculated to lead to the discovery of admissible evidence.

The frequency or extent of use of the discovery methods set forth in subdivision (a) shall be limited by the court if it determines that: (i) the discovery sought is unreasonably cumulative or duplicative, or is obtainable from some other source that is more convenient, less burdensome, or less expensive; (ii) the party seeking discovery has had ample opportunity by discovery in the action to obtain the information sought; or (iii) the discovery is unduly burdensome or expensive, taking into account the needs of the case, the amount in controversy, limitations on the parties' resources, and the importance of the issues at stake in the litigation. The court may act upon its own initiative after reasonable notice or pursuant to a motion under subdivision (c).

* * *

(c) Protective Orders. Upon motion by a party or by the person from whom discovery is sought, and for good cause shown, the court in which the action is pending or alternatively, on matters relating to a deposition, the court in the district where the deposition is to be taken may make any order which justice requires to protect a party or person from annoyance, embarrassment, oppression, or undue burden or expense, including one or more of the following: (1) that the discovery not be had; (2) that the discovery may be had only on specified terms and conditions, including a designation of the time or place; (3) that the discovery may be had only by a method of discovery other than that selected by the party seeking discovery; (4) that certain matters not be inquired into, or that the scope of the discovery be limited to certain matters; (5) that discovery be conducted with no one present except persons designated by the court; (6) that a deposition after being sealed be opened only by order of the court; (7) that a trade secret or other confidential research, development, or commercial information not be disclosed or be disclosed only in a designated way; (8) that the parties simultaneously file specified documents or information enclosed in sealed envelopes to be opened as directed by the court.

If the motion for a protective order is denied in whole or in part, the court may, on such terms and conditions as are just, order that any party or person provide or permit discovery. The provisions of Rule 37(a)(4) apply to the award of expenses incurred in relation to the motion.

(d) Sequence and Timing of Discovery. Unless the court upon motion, for the convenience of parties and witnesses and in the interests of justice, orders otherwise, methods of discovery may be used in any sequence and the fact that a party is conducting discovery, whether by deposition or otherwise, shall not operate to delay any other party's discovery.

(e) Supplementation of Responses. A party who has responded to a request for discovery with a response that was complete when made is under no duty to supplement the response to include information thereafter acquired, except as follows: (1) A party is under a duty seasonably to supplement the response with respect to any question directly addressed to (A) the identity and location of persons having knowledge of discoverable matters, and (B) the identify of each person expected to be called as an expert witness at trial, the subject matter on which the person is expected to testify, and the substance of the person's testimony. (2) A party is under a duty seasonably to amend a prior response if the party obtains information upon the basis of which (A) the party knows that the response was incorrect when made, or (B) the party knows that the response though correct when made is no longer true and the circumstances are such that a failure to amend the response is in substance a knowing concealment. (3) A duty to supplement responses may be imposed by order of the court, agreement of the parties, or at any time prior to trial through new requests for supplementation of prior responses.

(f) Discovery Conference. At any time after commencement of an action the court may direct the attorneys for the parties to appear before it for a conference on the subject of discovery. The court shall do so upon motion by the attorney for any party if the motion includes: (1) A statement of the issues as they then appear; (2) A proposed plan and schedule of discovery; (3) Any limitations proposed to be placed on discovery; (4) Any other proposed orders with respect to discovery; and (5) A statement showing that the attorney making the motion has made a reasonable effort to reach agreement with opposing attorneys on the matters set forth in the motion. Each party and each party's attorney are under a duty to participate in good faith in the framing of a discovery plan if a plan is proposed by the attorney for any party. Notice of the motion shall be served on all parties. Objections or additions to matters set forth in the motion shall be served not later than 10 days after service of the motion.

Following the discovery conference, the court shall enter an order tentatively identifying the issues for discovery purposes, establishing a plan and schedule for discovery, setting limitations on discovery, if any; and determining such other matters, including the allocation of expenses, as are necessary for the proper management of discovery in the action. An order may be altered or amended whenever justice so requires.

Subject to the right of a party who properly moves for a discovery conference to prompt convening of the conference, the court may combine the discovery conference with a pretrial conference authorized by Rule 16.

(g) Signing of Discovery Requests, Responses, and Objections. Every request for discovery or response or objection thereto made by a party represented by an attorney shall be signed by at least one attorney of record in the attorney's individual name, whose address shall be stated. A party who is not represented by an attorney shall sign the request, response, or objection and state the party's address. The signature of the attorney or party constitutes a certification that the signer has read the request, response, or objection, and that to the best of the signer's knowledge, information, and belief formed after a reasonable inquiry it is: (1) consistent with these rules and warranted by existing law or a good faith argument for the extension, modification, or reversal of existing law; (2) not interposed for any improper purpose, such as to harass or to cause unnecessary delay or needless increase in the cost of litigation; and (3) not unreasonable or unduly burdensome or expensive, given the needs of the case, the discovery already had in the case, the amount in controversy, and the importance of the issues at stake in the litigation. If a request, response, or objection is not signed, it shall be stricken unless it is signed promptly after the omission is called to the attention of the party making the request, response, or objection, and a party shall not be obligated to take any action with respect to it until it is signed.

If a certification is made in violation of the rule, the court, upon motion or upon its own initiative, shall impose upon the person who made the certification, the party on whose behalf the request, response, or objection is made, or both, an appropriate sanction, which may include an order to pay the amount of the reasonable expenses incurred because of the violation, including a reasonable attorney's fee.

Rule 50. Motion for a Directed Verdict and for Judgment Notwithstanding the Verdict

(a) Motion for Directed Verdict: When Made; Effect. A party who moves for a directed verdict at the close of the evidence offered by an opponent may offer evidence in the event that the motion is not granted, without having reserved the right so to do and to the same extent as if the motion had not been made. A motion for a directed verdict which is not granted is not a waiver of trial by jury even though all parties to the action have moved for directed verdicts. A motion for a directed verdict shall state the specific grounds therefor. The order of the court granting a motion for a directed verdict is effective without any assent of the jury.

(b) Motion for Judgment Notwithstanding the Verdict. Whenever a motion for a directed verdict made at the close of all the evidence is denied or for any reason is not granted, the court is deemed to have submitted the action to the jury subject to a later determination of the legal questions raised by the motion. Not later than 10 days after entry of judgment, a party who has moved for a directed verdict may move to have the verdict and any judgment entered thereon set aside and to have judgment entered in accordance with the party's motion for a directed verdict; or if a verdict was not returned such party, within 10 days after the jury has been discharged, may move for judgment in accordance with the party's motion for a directed verdict. A motion for a new trial may be joined with this motion, or a new trial may be prayed for in the alternative. If a verdict was returned the court may allow the judgment to stand or may reopen the judgment and either order a new trial or direct the entry of judgment as if the requested verdict had been directed. If no verdict was returned the court may direct the entry of judgment as if the requested verdict had been directed or may order a new trial.

(c) Same: Conditional Rulings on Grant of Motion. (1) If the motion for judgment notwithstanding the verdict, provided for in subdivision (b) of this rule, is granted, the court shall also rule on the motion for a new trial, if any, by determining whether it should be granted if the judgment is thereafter vacated or reversed, and shall specify the grounds for granting or denying the motion for the new trial. If the motion for a new trial is thus conditionally granted, the order thereon does not affect the finality of the judgment. In case the motion for a new trial has been conditionally granted and the judgment is reversed on appeal, the new trial shall proceed unless the appellate court has otherwise ordered. In case the motion for a new trial has been conditionally denied, the appellee on appeal may assert error in that denial; and if the judgment is reversed on appeal, subsequent proceedings shall be in accordance with the order of the appellate court. (2) The party whose verdict has been set aside on motion for judgment notwithstanding the verdict may serve a motion for a new trial pursuant to Rule 59 not later than 10 days after entry of the judgment notwithstanding the verdict.

(d) Same: Denial of Motion. If the motion for judgment notwithstanding the verdict is denied, the party who prevailed on that motion may, as appellee, assert grounds entitling the party to a new trial in the event the appellate court concludes that the trial court erred in denying the motion for judgment notwithstanding the verdict. If the appellate court reverses the judgment, nothing in this rule precludes it from determining that the appellee is entitled to a new trial, or from directing the trial court to determine whether a new trial shall be granted.

Rule 56. Summary Judgment

(a) **For Claimant.** A party seeking to recover upon a claim, counter-claim, or cross-claim or to obtain a declaratory judgment may, at any time after the expiration of 20 days from the commencement of the action or after service of a motion for summary judgment by the adverse party, move with or without supporting affidavits for a summary judgment in the party's favor upon all or any part thereof.

(b) **For Defending Party.** A party against whom a claim, counter-claim, or cross-claim is asserted or a declaratory judgment is sought may, at any time, move with or without supporting affidavits for a summary judgment in the party's favor as to all or any part thereof.

(c) **Motion and Proceedings Thereon.** The motion shall be served at least 10 days before the time fixed for the hearing. The adverse party prior to the day of hearing may serve opposing affidavits. The judgment sought shall be rendered forthwith if the pleadings, depositions, answers to interrogatories, and admissions on file, together with the affidavits, if any, show that there is no genuine issue as to any material fact and that the moving party is entitled to a judgment as a matter of law. A summary judgment, interlocutory in character, may be rendered on the issue of liability alone although there is a genuine issue as to the amount of damages.

(d) **Case Not Fully Adjudicated on Motion.** If on motion under this rule judgment is not rendered upon the whole case or for all the relief asked and a trial is necessary, the court at the hearing of the motion, by examining the pleadings and the evidence before it and by interrogating counsel, shall if practicable ascertain what material facts exist without substantial controversy and what material facts are actually and in good faith controverted. It shall thereupon make an order specifying the facts that appear without substantial controversy, including the extent to which the amount of damages or other relief is not in controversy, and directing such further proceedings in the action as are just. Upon the trial of the action the facts so specified shall be deemed established, and the trial shall be conducted accordingly.

(e) **Form of Affidavits; Further Testimony; Defense Required.** Supporting and opposing affidavits shall be made on personal knowledge, shall set forth such facts as would be admissible in evidence, and shall show affirmatively that the affiant is competent to testify to the matters stated therein. Sworn or certified copies of all papers or parts thereof referred to in an affidavit shall be attached thereto or served therewith. The court may permit affidavits to be supplemented or opposed by depositions, answers to interrogatories, or further affidavits. When a motion for summary judgment is made and supported as provided in this rule, an adverse party may not rest upon the mere allegations or denials of the adverse party's pleading, but the adverse party's response, by affidavits or as otherwise provided in this rule, must set forth specific facts showing that there is a genuine issue for trial. If the adverse party does not so respond, summary judgment, if appropriate, shall be entered against the adverse party.

(f) When Affidavits are Unavailable. Should it appear from the affidavits of a party opposing the motion that the party cannot for reasons stated present by affidavit facts essential to justify the party's opposition, the court may refuse the application for judgment or may order a continuance to permit affidavits to be obtained or depositions to be taken or discovery to be had or may make such other order as is just.

(g) Affidavits Made in Bad Faith. Should it appear to the satisfaction of the court at any time that any of the affidavits presented pursuant to this rule are presented in bad faith or solely for the purpose of delay, the court shall forthwith order the party employing them to pay to the other party the amount of the reasonable expenses which the filing of the affidavits caused the other party to incur, including reasonable attorney's fees, and any offending party or attorney may be adjudged guilty of contempt.

Rule 59. New Trials; Amendment of Judgments

(a) Grounds. A new trial may be granted to all or any of the parties and on all or part of the issues (1) in an action in which there has been a trial by jury, for any of the reasons for which new trials have heretofore been granted in actions at law in the courts of the United States; and (2) in an action tried without a jury, for any of the reasons for which rehearings have heretofore been granted in suits in equity in the courts of the United States. On a motion for a new trial in an action tried without a jury, the court may open the judgment if one has been entered, take additional testimony, amend findings of fact and conclusions of law or make new findings and conclusions, and direct the entry of a new judgment.

(b) Time for Motion. A motion for a new trial shall be served not later than 10 days after the entry of the judgment.

(c) Time for Serving Affidavits. When a motion for a new trial is based upon affidavits they shall be served with the motion. The opposing party has 10 days after such service within which to serve opposing affidavits, which period not exceeding 20 days either by the court for good cause shown or by the parties by written stipulation. The court may permit reply affidavits.

(d) On Initiative of Court. Not later than 10 days after entry of judgment the court of its own initiative may order a new trial for any reason for which it might have granted a new trial on motion of a party. After giving the parties notice and an opportunity to be heard on the matter, the court may grant a motion for a new trial, timely served, for a reason not stated in the motion. In either case, the court shall specify in the order the grounds therefor.

(e) Motion to Alter or Amend a Judgment. A motion to alter or amend the judgment shall be served not later than 10 days after entry of the judgment.

Rule 60. Relief From Judgment or Order

(a) Clerical Mistakes. Clerical mistakes in judgments, orders or other parts of the record and errors therein arising from oversight or omission may be corrected by the court at any time of its own initiative or on the motion of any party and after such notice, if any, as the court orders. During the pendency of an appeal, such mistakes may be so corrected before the appeal is docketed in the appellate court, and thereafter while the appeal is pending may be so corrected with leave of the appellate court.

(b) Mistakes; Inadvertence; Excusable Neglect; Newly Discovered Evidence; Fraud, etc. On motion and upon such terms as are just, the court may relieve a party or a party's legal representative from a final judgment, order, or proceeding for the following reasons: (1) mistake, inadvertence, surprise, or excusable neglect; (2) newly discovered evidence which by due diligence could not have been discovered in time to move for a new trial under Rule 59(b); (3) fraud (whether heretofore denominated intrinsic or extrinsic), misrepresentation, or other misconduct of an adverse party; (4) the judgment is void; (5) the judgment has been satisfied, released, or discharged, or a prior judgment upon which it is based has been reversed or otherwise vacated, or it is no longer equitable that the judgment should have prospective application; or (6) any other reason justifying relief from the operation of the judgment. The motion shall be made within a reasonable time, and for reasons (1), (2), and (3) not more than one year after the judgment, order, or proceeding was entered or taken. A motion under this subdivision (b) does not affect the finality of a judgment or suspend its operation. This rule does not limit the power of a court to entertain an independent action to relieve a party from a judgment, order, or proceeding, or to grant relief to a defendant not actually personally notified as provided in Title 28, U.S.C., 1655, or to set aside a judgment for fraud upon the court.

Rule 65. Injunctions

(a) Preliminary Injunction. (1) Notice. No preliminary injunction shall be issued without notice to the adverse party. (2) Consolidation of Hearing With Trial on Merits. Before or after the commencement of the hearing of an application for a preliminary injunction, the court may order the trial of the action on the merits to be advanced and consolidated with the hearing of the application. Even when this consolidation is not ordered, any evidence received upon an application for a preliminary injunction which would be admissible upon the trial on the merits becomes part of the record on the trial and need not be repeated upon the trial. This subdivision (a)(2) shall be so construed and applied as to save to the parties any rights they may have to trail by jury.

(b) Temporary Restraining Order; Notice; Hearing; Duration. A temporary restraining order may be granted without written or oral notice to the adverse party or that party's attorney only if (1) it clearly appears from specific facts shown by affidavit or by the verified complaint that immediate and irreparable injury, loss, or damage will result to the applicant before the adverse party or that party's attorney can be heard in opposition, and (2) the applicant's attorney certifies to the court in writing the efforts, if any, which have been made to give the notice and the reasons supporting the claim that notice should not be required. Every temporary restraining order granted without notice shall be endorsed with the date and hour of issuance; shall be filed forthwith in the clerk's office and entered of record; shall define the injury and state why it is irreparable and why the order was granted without notice; and shall expire by its terms within such time after entry, not to exceed 10 days, as the court fixes, unless within the time so fixed the order, for good cause shown, is extended for a like period or unless the party against whom the order is directed consents that it may be extended for a longer period. The reasons for the extension shall be entered of record. In case a temporary restraining order is granted without notice, the motion for a preliminary injunction shall be set down for hearing at the earliest possible time and takes precedence of all matters except older matters of the same character; and when the motion comes on for hearing the party who obtained the temporary restraining order shall proceed with the application for a preliminary injunction and, if the party does not do so, the court shall dissolve the temporary restraining order. On 2 days' notice to the party who obtained the temporary restraining order without notice or on such shorter notice to that party as the court may prescribe, the adverse party may appear and move its dissolution or modification and in the event the court shall proceed to hear and determine such motion as expeditiously as the ends of justice require.

(c) Security. No restraining order or preliminary injunction shall issue except upon the giving of security by the application, in such sum as the court deems proper, for the payment of such costs and damages as may be incurred or suffered by any party who is found to have been wrongfully enjoined or restrained. No such security shall be required of the United States or of an officer or agency thereof ... .

(d) Form and Scope of Injunction or Restraining Order. Every order granting an injunction and every restraining order shall set forth the reasons for its issuance; shall be specific in terms; shall describe in reasonable detail, and not by reference to the complaint or other document, the act or acts sought to be restrained; and is binding only upon the parties to the action, their officers, agents, servants, employees, and attorneys, and upon those persons in active concert or participation with them who received actual notice of the order by personal service or otherwise.

Index